THE QUOTABLE CLIMBER

THE QUOTABLE CLIMBER

*Literary, Humorous, Inspirational,
and Fearful Moments of Climbing*

EDITED BY JONATHAN WATERMAN

THE LYONS PRESS

Photographs on pages 27, 71, 97, 117, 167, 177, 187, and 197 by
Ed Webster / Mountain Imagery. All Rights Reserved.
Photograph on page 153 courtesy of Aldo Audisio
Other photographs by Jonathan Waterman.

Design by Joel Friedlander, Marin Bookworks

Printed in the United States of America

10 9 8 7 6 5 4 3 2 1

Library of Congress Cataloging-in-Publication Data

The quotable climber: literary, humorous, inspirational, and fearful
moments of climbing / edited by Johnathan Waterman
     p.   cm.
   ISBN 1–55821–718–5
   1. Mountaineering—Quotations, maxims, etc.
  2. Mountaineers—Quotations.   I. Waterman, Johnathan.
  GV200.Q68   1998
796.52'2—dc21   98–17992
                                          CIP

To June Duell

CONTENTS

INTRODUCTION

If someone asks why you climb, don't say "because it's there." This was the mistake I made trying to explain the game to my parents. Like most guardians of adolescents, they thought that their child's climbing was some manifestation of a death wish. Mostly I pulled up shy of explanations. I checked out books from the library and sought to expand upon why I climbed: what made it beautiful, how the large planet became more accessible (through its mountain ranges and climbing areas), how my circle of friends enlarged, how my fears were defined, and why one could dedicate much of one's life to such a seemingly inexplicable and even dangerous pastime. It never occurred to me to simply show my parents the height and breadth of climbing books contained in our suburban Boston library.

On one level, I wanted to communicate the sublimity of the climbing experience. But it was mostly my exasperation that compelled me to write about climbing. I wanted to dispel the notion of climbing as a crazy, misanthropic, macho, or eccentric act. Undoubtedly, many climbers become writers because of the misconceptions about climbing (although you won't hear any climbing writer admitting this). If climbing

were merely an accepted and televised sport—in which the
spectators never asked *why*—the literature would not be so *tall*.

When I worked as a naturalist, then a mountain guide,
I had a mimeographed scrapbook of quotes. They were culled
from various books, magazines, and overheard conversations.
Finally, I thought: a shortcut for those students and my parents (and me) who were all struggling to understand the philosophy behind climbing. I kept the thumb-worn scrapbook
until it had all but disintegrated from countless trips, accompanying friends and amateurs through the mountains. When
my own ideas or inspiration foundered, I simply pulled out
the scrapbook and read a snippet of Walter Bonatti (for spiritualism), Reinhold Messner (to explain the philosophy of
climbing light), Tom Patey (to get people laughing), Henry
David Thoreau (to show the sanctity of nature), or Royal
Robbins (for technique).

Now, with a prod from an editor (Bryan Oettel) and my
agent (Susan Golomb), I have expanded and modernized that
scrapbook. I would like to believe that I have created an inspirational reference for experts and neophytes, curious parents
and students, believers and nonbelievers. There was one last
surprise, too. While researching *The Quotable Climber*, I
found (and rediscovered) those words and explanations that
allowed me to more carefully define my own motives, even
though I now merely launch out on occasional expeditions.
Nonetheless, exploring and examining one's motives—vis-à-
vis the experiences of others—should be an essential founda-

tion for climbing. In the words of Socrates, who, unfortunately, was born too long ago to climb:

"The unexamined life is not worth living."

≍

Depending upon whose statistics you read, anywhere from two hundred thousand to a half million people actively climb today in North America. Add to this at least another quarter of a million people who used to climb, who want to learn how to climb, or who simply peruse the climbing literature for vicarious thrills.

While these numbers won't support climbing as a legitimate mainstream sport or Olympic event—such as golf, skiing, football, or tennis—why is it that the literature of climbing, stacked cover-to-cover, would tower over those other mainstream sports books like the Himalayas over the Appalachians? Partly because climbing is an older sport. But mostly because conventional athletes rarely, if ever, die on the playing field. Jon Krakauer's *Into Thin Air* would *not* have become a best-seller without that most haunting of all literary themes: death (body count from that book is eight men and women). Certainly, I found no shortage of death-related quotes for the Great Divide chapter.

Still, it would be disingenuous to suggest that the literature is only tall because of epitaphs. The literature is tall because good writers like Krakauer and Heinrich Harrer and Elizabeth Knowlton and Geoffrey Winthrop Young and Maurice Herzog and Alison Osius and David Roberts and

Wilfrid Noyce and Lionel Terray and Joe Simpson and Peter Boardman and Greg Child and Gaston Rébuffat and Steve Roper and Miriam Underhill and H. W. Tilman and Jeff Long and Eric Shipton have all communicated about climbing. Some of them undoubtedly wrote out of exasperation; many of them did it to share the sublimity of their experiences. These writers have explained: The Great Divide, Commitment and Desire, Camaraderie, Decadence and Revelry, Outsiders, Risk and Luck, Famous Climbs, Summits, Female Inspiration, the Greatest Hill on Earth, Gearing Up, Getting Gripped, Female Inspiration, Accidents and Epics, Hubris, Humility, Looking Back, and Why.

One phenomenon of modern climbing is that many of the top athletes (infrequent writers) are strangely oblivious to this massive mountain range of literature or its history. Ask the average sport climber who Fritz Wiessner, Gaston Rébuffat, or Miriam Underhill were, and, usually, he or she will know more about athletes Babe Ruth, Wilt Chamberlain, or Billie Jean King. Or, take the example of one well-known alpinist who published in *Climbing* magazine. He wrote that no one had ever climbed in his own fast and lightweight style in the Alaska Range. In fact it had been done (and written about) countless times before, beginning in 1910, when the wool-sweatered Sourdoughs climbed 10,000 feet up Denali in a single day, equipped with only thermos, doughnuts, and a fourteen-foot spruce pole.

Another one of my agendas is now plain. Others have gone before us. We are not alone; we are rarely first.

To quote Santayana:

"Those who can't remember the past are condemned to repeat it."

≍

I have a collection of more than five hundred books that runs the gamut. Novels, guidebooks, coffee table tomes, history books, biographies, and nonfiction narratives. The truth is, at least a hundred are climbing books. More tallness, standing alongside Matthiessen, McCarthy, O'Brien, Hemingway, and Steinbeck. Stacked cover to cover, the climbing books pile from the floor to the ceiling, then back again. This is where I began mining quotes.

I continued digging among the fourteen thousand volumes at the American Alpine Club Library and various other public and university libraries, sifting through not only books, but a wide array of magazines (especially *Climbing*), journals, the Internet, remembered lectures, even videotapes. Climbers, no one would be surprised to learn, have a lot to say.

Outside of the many technique-craft-how-to books and articles, and shy of taking a recorder to the various climbing arenas for the next ten years, there is a distinct dearth of quotes describing the actual climbing. And these rare descriptions of the ballet of climbing aren't nearly as illuminating and succinct as those humorous or understated descriptions of the friendships, the fright, the narcissism, the rationale, or the all-around spiritualism of climbing. I included more than six hundred quotes; I left out thousands more. If you think that I may have overlooked important quotes, please send them to the publisher for inclusion in a future edition.

Initially I separated the various disciplines of climbing—sport, rock, ice, alpinism—into their own chapters, until it became apparent that the various practitioners were all talking about the same idea. The essential romanticism and motivation and discipline of climbing are not altogether different whether you're busting a move at the ceiling of a gym, slotting a hand crack, hooking chandelier ice, or sucking air at 8,000 meters. As that Descartes paraphrase of the collective climbing community goes:

"We climb, therefore we are."

THE QUOTABLE CLIMBER

CAMARADERIE

"When men climb on a great mountain together, the rope between them is more than a mere physical aid to the ascent; it is a symbol of the spirit of the enterprise. It is a symbol of men banded together in a common effort of will and strength against their only true enemies: inertia, cowardice, greed, ignorance, and all weaknesses of the spirit."

—Charles Houston

CAMARADERIE

One need merely attend one of the annual meetings of the American Alpine Club (held each year in a different city) in order to see the inner workings of friendship among climbers. Men and women gather together and celebrate one another's accomplishments throughout a long weekend of banquets, lectures, book signings, and award ceremonies. It is not uncommon to see spry octogenarians and twenty-something athletes embracing one another, exchanging addresses, and recounting the nuances of a faraway climb.

Although climbers of such stature as the great French alpinist, Lionel Terray, wrote in his book, *Conquistadors of the Useless*, that "mountaineering is an essentially individual experience, and I have always considered absurd the opinion, voiced by some authors, that the forging of bonds of friendship is its primary motivation," his famous friendship with Louis Lachenal, and the writings of another partner—Gaston Rébuffat—seem to refute Terray.

Solo climbing probably remains an uncommon pursuit because most climbers prefer not only the safety of the rope, but sharing the experience with a close friend. Some of the luminaries of climbing are known for their "fallouts"— Reinhold Messner and Peter Habeler disbanding after climbing Everest, Henry Barber abandoning Rob Taylor on Kilimanjaro, or Simon Yates cutting Joe Simpson's rope. Such rancorous stories remain the exceptions, however, because the world of climbing is mostly known for its heroic acts of companionship and selfless rescues.

One handful of influential climbers who remained friends for half a century are Charles Houston, Bob Bates, Bradford Washburn, Ad Carter, and Terris Moore. They all started climbing with one another at Harvard, then went on to set the standards for modern North American expeditionary climbers with first ascents throughout Alaska, the Alps, and the Himalaya. Houston and Bates in particular showed the modern world of mountaineering the meaning of true camaraderie on their 1953 K2 climb. They and five others risked their lives to evacuate the stricken Art Gilkey, who was miraculously swept off the mountain in an avalanche, an act of providence that probably saved everyone else's lives.

Washburn, like Bates and Houston, is still an active, eighty-seven-year-old traveler. He is renowned for helping Alaskan climbers with his photographs and route advice. Once, in an interview, he summed up camaraderie: "I wouldn't last for thirty minutes climbing solo."

▲ ▲ ▲

"The least slip on the part of my companion and I should be dead. . . . yet I was more worried about my own possible clumsiness than his."

—**Lionel Terray**, on steep ice with Gaston Rébuffat.

≍

"I've climbed with some of the best climbers in the world, more importantly, to me, they are some of the best people in the world. That's another reason why I climb."

—**Jim Wickwire**

≍

"Mack the Knife."

—**Simon Yates's** nickname after cutting the rope to Joe Simpson during their South American climb.

≍

"Nations touch at their summits."

—**Walter Bagehot**, 1826–1877, British journalist.

≍

"They are the links that remind me that I would let everyone down if I fell—and they don't care what route I do."

—**Guy Lacelle,** ice soloist, talking about his dogs.

"He does not climb for himself, he throws open the gates of his mountains as a gardener opens the gates of his garden. The heights are a splendid setting for his work, and the climbing gives him a pleasure of which he never tires. But above all he is repaid by the pleasure of the man he guides. He knows that such-and-such a climb is particularly beautiful and that this ice ridge is delicate as lace. He says nothing of all this but his reward is in his companion's smile of discovery."

—**Gaston Rébuffat**

≍

"Good looks a plus. SWF 19 humorous caring considerate, enjoys roller blading, swimming, rock climbing, reading, biking, seek sweet trustworthy SM Call 1-900-XXX-XXXX extension 8255"

—Vancouver personals.

≍

"To all who knew Willi and loved him."

—**Tom Hornbein's** dedication to Willi Unsoeld in the 1980 edition of *Everest: The West Ridge*.

≍

"We so far forgot ourselves as to shake hands."

—**H. W. Tilman,** summiting the highest peak yet climbed, Nanda Devi, with Noel Odell in 1936.

"Seilschaft" [which translates from German as *insider relationship*].

> —**Heinrich Harrer,** upon being asked what his most significant accomplishments were.

≍

"When the pursuit of natural harmony is a shared journey, great heights can be attained."

—Lynn Hill

≍

"I stopped a half dozen steps short, belayed David up, and we took the last steps together."

> —**Todd Thompson,** on the North Ridge of Mount Kennedy, 1968.

≍

"You Americans disgust me."

> —Soloist **Reinhold Messner,** *sotto voce* to eight Americans on Denali's West Buttress Route.

"We reached the summit almost together."

> —From the press statement that **Edmund Hillary** and
> Sherpa **Tenzing Norgay** signed in 1953 to dispel
> questions about who first reached the summit of
> Everest.

≍

"How beautiful this would be if I could only share it with
someone."

> —French water colorist **Samovel's** caption for a lone
> man staring out at a mountain sunset.

≍

"If there is a deeper and more lasting message behind our venture than the mere passing sensation of a physical feat, I believe
this to be the value of comradeship and the many virtues
which combine to create it. Comradeship, regardless of race or
creed, is forged among high mountains, through the difficulties and dangers to which they expose those who aspire to
climb them, the need to combine the efforts to attain their
goal, the thrills of a great adventure shared together."

> **—Sir John Hunt**

"The mountain is nothing without people on it. Often you part expeditions exasperated, but a year or two later, you go back with the same partners knowing there's potential in this human relationship."

>   —**Greg Child**

≍

"Long live the crew."

>   —**Jake Breitenbach**

≍

"The camaraderie of the rope."

>   —**Chris Bonington,** who forgot his rope for a climbing
>   interview with a journalist and a television crew,
>   explaining to them how he could so easily borrow the
>   only rope from two nearby strangers (read *fans*)
>   preparing to embark upon their own climb.

≍

"Mountaineering transcends all everyday matters. It transcends all natural frontiers. Mountaineers are bands of brothers. They are all one party on one rope."

>   —**Guido Tonella,** writing in 1946 about reuniting
>   Europe.

"Together we knew toil, joy, and pain. My fervent wish is that the nine of us who were united in face of death should remain fraternally united through life."

> —**Maurice Herzog,** writing about the 1950 expedition to Annapurna.

"Among us there is no team spirit, only a necessary politeness. What hypocrisy!"

> —**Gaston Rébuffat** writing about the 1950 expedition to Annapurna.

SOLO

"For many hours I have only used up energy. I have climbed myself to a standstill, now I am experiencing regeneration, a return flow of energy."

—**Reinhold Messner,** squatting on top of the world, during his extraordinary oxygen-free solo.

SOLO

Soloing is the antithesis of camaraderie. Given the origins of climbing in the smoking parlor fraternities of the privileged, it is no small wonder that soloists are decried as the heretics of climbing. Soloing is partly about being a renegade. It is about cutting the umbilical of rope and companionship, and going into a meditative state beyond the normal realities of both climbing and life.

Native American folklore describes vision quests in which lone men would fast and journey up mountains in order to find meaning for their lives. In modern times, there are more than a few psychiatrists who submit that "alone time" is a biological need, vital for creating healthy relationships, lasting careers, and allowing one to find a niche in society. Tell these same shrinks about climbing alone, without a rope, and they will tell you that you're suicidal. Soloing can indeed be harebrained—even most climbers support the oft-repeated dictum, "If you fall, you die."

Nonetheless. The most influential alpinist of the twentieth century also happens to be one of the most amazing soloists: Reinhold Messner. And the only occasion he has been seriously injured soloing was the time he forgot his house key and was forced to solo up over a forty-foot wall to get into his castle: He fell and hit the ground spraining his ankle. The rest of his solos—numerous speed ascents in the Alps such as a visionary 1969 dash up the North Face of Les Droites, then a bold climb of the eight-thousand-meter

Nanga Parbat, and finally his oxygen-free sprint up Everest—stretched the definition of *possible* and allowed most climbers to rethink the conventions. *If you fall, you die;* but maybe . . . if you *don't* fall . . .

Messner, of course, had inspirations. In 1953, Austrian climber Hermann Buhl reached the summit of Nanga Parbat without his teammates (then was killed soloing in the Himalaya a few years later). In the 1960s, Italian climber Walter Bonatti broke psychological barriers for climbers everywhere by soloing the Southwest Face of the Dru and the North Face of the Matterhorn. The torch was carried throughout the rock climbing world in the 1970s by Henry Barber with a series of bold and unroped rock climbs—in particular, his 1971 on-sight solo of the Steck-Salathé route in Yosemite.

Ultimately, there are altogether too many soloists to name cohesively. One of the first, if only in spirit, for his lone ascent of Katahdin in the nineteenth century (before the Appalachian Mountain Club was formed) was the renegade New Englander, Henry David Thoreau. By deliberately isolating himself and capturing the experience with his writing, Thoreau inspired several generations of mountain goers and nature lovers to seek solitude. Of those more recent climbing soloists—Derrick Hershey, John Bachar, Mugs Stump, Jeff Lowe, John Mallon Waterman, and Henry Barber—it should not escape the reader's attention that half of them died in the mountains.

▲ ▲ ▲

"This stillness, solitude, wildness of nature is a kind of thoroughwort or boneset, to my intellect. This is what I go out to seek. It is as if I always met in those places some grand, serene, immortal, infinitely encouraging though invisible, companion, and walked with him."

—Henry David Thoreau

≍

"We have your application to make a solo climb of Mt. McKinley. You have a great deal of climbing experience and I'm sure [you] realize the risks involved in climbing a [mountain] such as McKinley alone. We cannot authorize you to do so."

—1970 Park Service letter to Naomi Uemura, who sneaked on the mountain and completed the first solo.

"In all the splendor of solitude . . . it is a test of myself, and one thing I loathe is to have to test myself in front of other people."

—Naomi Uemura

"Solitude is a silent storm that breaks down all our dead branches. Yet it sends our living roots deeper into the living heart of the living earth. Man struggles to find life outside himself, unaware that the life he is seeking is within him. Nature reaches out to us with welcoming arms, and bids us enjoy her beauty; but we dread her silence and rush into the crowded cities, there to huddle like sheep fleeing from a ferocious wolf."

> —**Kahlil Gibran**

≍

"Tell Webster's to change the definition of insanity to 'John Bachar solos New Dimensions'."

> —Yosemite's Camp 4 bulletin board in 1979.

≍

"I like to be alone in the peace of nature. The joy of nature."

> —**Fritz Wiessner,** in his seventies, on soloing hundreds of easier fifth-class routes in the Gunks.

≍

"Probably the hardest climb done by man."

> —**Mugs Stump's** half-facetious comment on his solo of Antarctica's unclimbed, 8,200-foot West Face of Tyree, in thirty-below-zero temperatures in 1990.

"Some people love soloing and are great at it, and they can have it."

—**Alison Osius**

≍

"A lot of my soloing—although not my best—was done under duress, when I was upset about love or goals or something. You get to the point where you don't care as much."

—**Jim Erickson**

≍

"He always asks for more, more, more. He never gets enough. He is insatiable, gluttonous, ever lusting for more of the peculiar meat upon which he feeds."

—**Royal Robbins,** on the demon within that made
    him solo El Capitan's Muir Wall in Yosemite.

≍

"The idea behind my runouts on Paris Girl was that a good climber could climb 5.13 and solo 5.10."

—**Christian Griffith,** on his significant (and
    dangerous) new rock route.

"Maybe it was not this summer when I first heard the voices, but I think it was, because I know it was before I played with bows and arrows or rode a horse (four years old), and I was out playing alone when I heard them. It was like somebody calling me, and I thought it was my mother but there was nobody there. This happened more than once and always made me afraid, so that I ran home."

—**John Gneisenau Neihardt,** *Black Elk Speaks.*

≍

"My success rate is much higher when I'm soloing. It's easier to talk yourself into quitting when you have someone to talk to."

—**Amanda Tarr** (22), soloist of three Zion walls, and Black Canyon of the Gunnison's Painted Wall.

≍

"In Genesis it says that it is not good for a man to be alone, but sometimes it is a great relief."

—**John Barrymore,** American actor.

≍

"It's not really suicidal. But there's definitely a feeling of, *if I die, then she'll appreciate me.*"

—Anonymous male solo climber talking about his girlfriend.

"Living through it would mean that Nature wasn't as raw as everybody wanted to believe it was. Living through it would mean that Mount Hunter wasn't the mountain that I thought it was."

>   —**John Mallon Waterman,** after surviving a 148-day
>   solo of that mountain.

≍

"Flocks of birds have flown high and away.
A solitary drift of cloud, too, has gone,
>   wandering on.
And I sit alone with the Ching-Ting Peak,
>   towering beyond.
We never grow tired of each other,
>   the mountain and I."

>   —**Li Po,** A.D. 762

≍

"You wouldn't be givin' me double-talk now, wouldja, friend?"

>   —Logger **Jim Freeman,** on a remote Alaskan shoreline,
>   after meeting Jon Krakauer who just mentioned his
>   recent solo of the Devils Thumb.

"To feel themselves in the presence of true greatness many men find it necessary only to be alone."

—**Tom Masson**, American editor.

≍

"Progress in technique, training and equipment had made the climber too efficient; as in many another field, technique was in the process killing adventure. For those who sought to define their own nature, in the combat of man against the mountain, there would soon be no solution but the desperate ways of the solo climber and the winter mountaineer."

—**Lionel Terray**

≍

"The sensation is akin to coasting down the motorway after being held up at every set of traffic lights in Glasgow."

—**Tom Patey**

≍

"It is a fine thing to be out on the hills alone. A man can hardly be a beast or a fool alone on a great mountain."

—**Reverend Francis Kilvert**, 1886–1918.

"From the earliest glimmering of human consciousness we find an introvert view of life accompanying and complementing this extrovert view. Aristotle's definition of man as a 'social animal' is not sufficiently comprehensive."

—**Ernst Cassirer,** from *An Essay of Man.*

≍

"If you fall, you are dead."

—**Catherine Destivelle**

≍

"Men always talk of the conquest of mountains. And here he comes across the glacier, looks up only once, very slowly. He glances at me, comes on with sunken head, is no longer consciously there. Going up to him I say, 'Reinhold, how are you?' A few sobs are the answer."

—**Nena Holguin,** greeting her boyfriend after he soloed Everest.

SPIRITUALITY
AND NATURE

"I will lift mine eyes unto the hills, from whence cometh my help."

—Psalms, 121:1

SPIRITUALITY AND NATURE

Appreciating the beauties of crags and mountains, as well as meditating upon one's own soul while sitting on a belay ledge, might, until recently, have been the most treasured element of climbing. As the poet Barry wrote:

> I love the waste
> the open space
> where we taste
> the pleasure of believing
> that all we see
> is boundless
> as we wish
> our souls to be.

There are a myriad of climbers who, if not practicing Buddhists, embrace the ideals of Buddhism. In 1989, the Nobel Peace Prize was awarded to the Dalai Lama for his advocacy of peace and spiritual harmony between people and nature—e.g., mountains, rivers, and wildlife.

In a similar vein, climbing institutions such as the Access Fund, the Mountain Foundation, and the American Alpine Club all contribute to various environmental and conservation projects: building trails to prevent erosion, protecting raptor cliff nesting areas, and recognizing those who work toward conservation in climbing.

Although trashing out the mountains is now considered unethical, not all climbers are environmentally or spiritually attuned. There are many climbing areas—rock faces and mountainsides alike—still being desecrated by chipped holds, garbage, graffiti, abandoned oxygen cylinders, and bolts. Many modern climbers, who began their apprenticeships in gyms on artificial climbing holds, are often led to believe that climbing is a mere gymnastic and narcissistic event, and consequently, lacking the appreciation of landscape and wilderness, they are unaware of the spiritual and environmental dimensions of climbing (let alone its hazards or ethical parameters). In this regard, the newest generation of climbers will confront the greatest challenges. As the pursuit of extreme difficulty narrows climbers' focus toward completing a mathematical sequence of moves, what will become of the soul and temple of climbing?

▲ ▲ ▲

"One should not go into churches if one wants to breathe pure air."

—**Friedrich Nietzsche**

≍

"In effect, the visible mountain ladder, cloud-compelling and controlling rain and sun, added a third dimension, that of height, to the length and breadth of surface supporting man in the dawn of his intelligence. It gave a new measure to his concrete vision of earth. By so doing, by asserting the existence of a higher world and of a higher order inhabiting it, mountains became the first forces to lift the eyes and thoughts of our branch of animal life above the levels of difficult existence to the Perception of a region of spirit, located, as children would locate it, in the sky above."

—**Geoffrey Winthrop Young**

≍

"A man does not climb a mountain without bringing some of it away with him and leaving something of himself upon it."

—**Sir Martin Conway**

≍

"It's as close as we can come to flying."

—**Margaret Young,** aviator and alpinist.

"I live not in myself,
but I become Portion
of that around me;
and to me
High mountains are a
feeling, but
the hum
Of human cities
torture."

   —Lord Byron

⋈

"For how great the pleasure, how great, think you, are the joys of the spirit, touched as is fit it should be, in wondering at the mighty mass of mountains while gazing upon their immensity and, as it were, in lifting one's head among the clouds. In some way or other the mind is overturned by their dizzying heights and is caught up in contemplation of the Supreme Architect."

   —Conrad Gesner

⋈

"Come forth into the light of things. Let nature be your teacher."

   —William Wordsworth, English poet, 1770–1850.

"I'm sorry about being at the root of all this furor about bolting."

> —**David Brower,** environmentalist, speaking at a recent climbers' gathering about how he placed North America's first expansion bolt on Shiprock, in 1939.

≍

"That the supreme and most precious moment of human living however much they may appear to depend on the body and the senses, are primarily experiences of the spirit."

—**James Ramsey Ullman**

≍

"The Mountain is not something externally sublime; It has a great historic and spiritual meaning for us. It stands for us as the ladder of life. Nay, more; it is the ladder of the soul, and in a curious way the source of religion. From it came the Law, from it came the Gospel in the Sermon on the Mount. We may truly say that the highest religion is the Religion of the Mountain."

> —**Jan Smuts,** 1919 prime minister of South Africa.

≍

"The goal of life is living in agreement with nature."

> —**Zeno** of Elea, Greek philosopher, 490–430 B.C.

"You may read, mark, learn all Alpine scriptures; their inward digestion is the matter of a lifetime."

—H. E. G. Tydale

≍

"In the last camp near the summit, I had a very strange vision of all the human parts I am made of. It is very difficult to keep the vision, but I know that I could see a round picture with many pictures inside—not only of my body, but of my whole being. There was a lot of what my life has been, what I did these last years, like seeing my life and my body and my soul and my feelings inside a mandala. But I was not even sure if it was only mine or generally human, yours or anybody's, just a human being's."

—**Reinhold Messner,** high on Kangchenjunga.

≍

"I looked back to the summit of the mountain, which seemed but a cubit high in comparison with the height of human contemplation, were in not too often merged in the corruptions of the earth."

—**Petrarch,** the Italian poet, after climbing Mount
    Ventoux in 1335.

"Climbing is not a battle with the elements, nor against the law of gravity. It's a battle against oneself."

—**Walter Bonatti**

≍

"In his laborious efforts to attain mountain tops, where the air is lighter and purer, the climber gains new strength of limb. In the endeavor to overcome obstacles of the way, the soul trains itself to conquer difficulties; and the Spectacle of the vast horizon, which from the highest crest offers itself on all sides to the eyes, raises his spirit to the Divine Author and Sovereign of Nature."

—**Pope Pius XI**

≍

"There are men who go to admire the high places of mountains, the great waves of the sea, the wide currents of rivers, the circuit of the ocean, and the orbits of the shore—and who neglect themselves."

—**Augustine,** bishop of Hippo, from *Confessions.*

≍

"Each fresh peak ascended teaches something."

—**Sir Martin Conway**

"The most beautiful and profound emotion we can experience is the sensation of the mystical. It is the source of all true science and art. He to whom this emotion is a stranger, who can no longer wonder and stand rapt in awe, is as good as dead. To know that what is impenetrable to us really exists, manifesting itself as the highest wisdom and the most radiant beauty which our dull faculties can comprehend only in their most primitive forms—this knowledge, this feeling is at the centre of true religiousness."

> —**Albert Einstein**

≍

"The soul of man is lifted up, a wider nobler horizon is offered to his view; surrounded by such silent majesty he seems to hear the very voice of Nature, and to become her confidant, to whom she tells the most secret of her operations."

> —**Horace Bénédict de Saussure,** Swiss scientist, atop
> Mont Blanc in 1787.

≍

"The forces of mountains are sublime and far-reaching;
the ability to ride on the clouds is permeated by the mountains; and the ability to follow the wind
is inevitably liberated by the mountains."

> —**Dógen,** *The Mountains and Rivers Sutra.*

"The Stone grows old
Eternity is not for stones.
But I shall go down from this airy space, this swift white peace,
This stinging exultation;
And time will close about me, and my soul stir to the rhythm
of the daily round.
Yet, having known, life will not press so close,
And always I shall feel time ravel thin about me.
For once I stood
In the white windy presence of eternity."

   —Eunice Tietjens, American poet, 1884–1944.

≍

"We want clean expeditions more than we want clean-up
expeditions."

   —Mr. Shresta, Nepalese Ministry of Tourism.

≍

"We can never have enough of nature. We must be refreshed
by the sight of inexhaustible vigor, vast and titanic features."

   —John Muir

≍

"Mountains are earth's undecaying monuments."

   —Nathaniel Hawthorne

"When, O! a mighty arch appeared, rising above the Lyskamm, high into the sky pale, colourless, and noiseless, but perfectly sharp and defined, except where it was lost in the clouds, this unearthly apparition seemed like a vision from another world; and, almost appalled, we watched with amazement the gradual development of two vast crosses, one on either side. If the Taugwalders had not been the first to perceive it, I should have doubted my senses. They thought it had some connection with the accident, and I, after a while, that it might bear some relation to ourselves. But our movements had no effect upon it. The spectral forms remained motionless. It was a fearful and wonderful sight; unique in my experience, and impressive beyond description, coming at such a moment."

—**Edward Whymper,** after his companions fell and
died on the first ascent of the Matterhorn in 1865.

⌒

"There was no thought in any of us of their being mere clouds. They were as clear as crystal, sharp on the pure horizon sky, and already tinged with rose by the sinking sun. Infinitely beyond all that we had ever thought or dreamed—the seen walls of lost Eden could not have been more beautiful to us; not more awful, round heaven, the walls of sacred death."

—**John Ruskin,** on seeing the Alps for the first time.

"May our five senses be pure,
and may the weather on the honorable mountain be fine."

—Japanese pilgrim's motto.

≍

"The springs of enchantment lie within ourselves; they arise
from our sense of wonder, that most precious of gifts, the
birthright of every child."

—**Eric Shipton,** from the last paragraph of his
autobiography.

≍

"These are not the signs of a good mountaineer."

—Indian liaison officer **Harish C. Thakus** at a
trashed-out basecamp in the Himalayas.

"Who need be craving a world beyond this one?
Here, among men, are the Purple Hills!"

—Chinese poet

≍

"Climb the mountains and get their good tidings. Nature's
peace will flow into you as sunshine flows into trees. The
winds will blow their own freshness into you, and the storms
their energy, while cares will drop off like autumn leaves."

—**John Muir**

"From the moment that my eyes rested on the snow-clad Alps I worshipped their beauty and was filled with a passionate yearning to touch these shining snows, to climb to their heights of silence and solitude, and feel myself one with the mighty forces around me."

—**Freda Du Faur,** in New Zealand.

≍

"And the ark rested in the seventh month, on the seventeenth day of the month, upon the mountains of Ararat. And the waters decreased continually until the tenth month: in the tenth month, on the first day of the month, were the tops of the mountains seen."

—Genesis 8:1–5

≍

"Caution Radiation
Air, Water, and Land Contaminated
by Homestake Milling Co."

—Sign beneath the sacred Mount Taylor, on Navajo land.

≍

"Take only pictures; leave only footprints."

—Anonymous

"The mountains have done the spiritual side of me more good religiously, as well as in my body physically, than anything else in the world. No one knows who and what God is until he has seen some real mountaineering and climbing in the alps."

—**Reverend F. T. Wethered,** 1919 letter to the *Alpine Journal.*

≍

"Ever since a small boy, I have loved just to look at the mountains, to see them in different lights and from different angles, to feel their rough rock under my fingers and the breath of their winds against my feet. . . . I am in love with the mountains."

—**Wilfrid Noyce**

DECADENCE AND REVELRY

"Screwing is more enjoyable than drilling bolt holes!"

    —Warren Harding

DECADENCE AND REVELRY

The acclaimed climbing anthology *The Games Climbers Play* included Royal Robbins's review of Warren Harding's book *Downward Bound*. It was a wonderful contrast—the straight man Robbins passing judgement on a volume that reflected a much more profane facet of the North American climbing scene. Harding epitomized climbing as a game and freely indulged himself in whatever decadence or fun might be available to the lot of the wall climber. Harding's irreverent book, like a few other weird or hilarious titles (the Burgess brothers' *Book of Lies*, Patey's *One Man's Mountains*, or Newby's *A Short Walk in the Hindu Kush*) was quite simply *decadent*.

It would be hard to ignore that climbers are, for the most part, an anarchistic and individualistic body of men and women. Most climbers are strongly opinionated, indifferent to rules, outspoken, and inclined to break normal society's taboos of etiquette and propriety, as well as generally unheeding of the damage they inflict upon their own bodies—by the severity of climbing itself, or the severe partying that precedes and follows a climbing event. The plethoric accounts of debauchery, arrest, inebriation, bar time, drug experimentation, speeding, fisticuffs, sexual forthrightness, inappropriate dress, and intolerance of tourists from outside the "tribe" are enough to show that climbers (with the exception perhaps of those in training for climbing competitions) are very unlike other outdoorspeople. Compare the average climber to, say,

the average equestrian, angler, hunter, or runner, and the profile makes everyone else look pretty clean-cut by comparison.

In the late 1950s and throughout the 1960s, there was
an active band of East Coast degenerates known as the
Vulgarians. They generally dressed in strange bandanna hats
and nonconformist tee shirts, then became famous for not
dressing at all during their spate of nude ascents, highlighted
by the famous photograph of Dick Williams letting it all hang
out on Shockley's Ceiling, in the Shawangunks. They overturned conformist climbers' cars, or urinated on these same
conformists as they walked below. Ultimately, the Vulgarians
came to symbolize the ascension of skilled climbers from non-
professional backgrounds.

These unbathed climbing bohemians can still be found
today. They sleep in the back of their beat-up cars, lift uneaten
food from strangers' plates, scam free gear, steal library climbing books, act slothfully, curse vehemently, decry God, sleep
around, dress poorly, and drink prodigiously. But don't believe
me. Check out the climbing accomplishments of those teeto-
taling conservatives—versus the hard-living Jim Bridwells and
Fred Beckeys—then draw your own conclusions.

▲ ▲ ▲

"The manners of mountaineers are commonly savage, but they are rather produced by their situation than derived from their ancestors."

—**Samuel Johnson,** eighteenth-century English arbiter of style and taste.

≍

"Climbers have no sense of smell."

—Climber Conrad Anker's mother, **Helga,** about her son and partners returning home from trips.

≍

"I admit the hole in my hat. I have it still and I like to think that the hole was made by a small falling stone and not, as I suspect, by the point of an ice ax when it blew off my head. The breeches, patched at knees and seat owing to a deplorable style of progression in both ascent and descent due to some atavistic recollection of pre-sensibility in the hinder organ, were confiscated years ago by stern female relations."

—**Sir Leslie Stephen**

≍

"I never have liked it when I had to stop laughing."

—**Tim Lewis,** telling why he wasn't a "serious" climber.

"This is the kind of book climbers steal from libraries."

> —**Paul Piana,** talking about his coffee-table book, *Big Walls: Breakthroughs on the Free-Climbing Frontier.*

≍

"This is the fucking life! No?"

> —**Jean Afanassieff,** famed French alpinist, on his mountain lifestyle.

≍

"It used to be said on the Pacific Coast of North America that the meanest thing any white man had ever done was taking home washing for a Chinaman; but what is that compared with a professor of Greek and a Poet carrying up soap, candles, and petroleum for a party of Alpinists?"

> —**Edward Whymper,** writing about the Duke of Abruzzi hiring ten American porters for Mount St. Elias.

≍

"Aren't you the lunger?"

> —**Diana Hunter** to Bob Williams

"I prefer to be called a swinger."

> —**Bob Williams** to Diana Hunter

"A short ice slope separated us from the crest, but we decided to abandon one of our bags, and the wine and major part of the supplies. Lightened by such drastic measures, we spiritedly attacked the rock teeth."

> —**Albert F. Mummery,** on the Matterhorn's Zmutt Ridge in 1894.

≍

"It is questionable whether poetry in the German language or physics textbooks qualify as general interest reading. While the writer makes no moral judgment of the practice, books emphasizing sex and violence are always popular."

> —**Boyd Everett,** on climbers' literary tastes.

≍

"Slug mode is when you lay in the tent with nothin' to do, maybe not even a book to read, maybe not even nothin' to eat. I can do it pretty well."

> —**Kitty Calhoun**

≍

"Why don't the rangers *do* something?"

> —An unidentified camper in Yosemite Valley, after the hungry Jeff Foott had stolen bacon from an ice chest in the middle of the night, while growling like a bear and leaving behind piton claw marks in the dirt.

"There will be plenty to eat and drink on the grounds, with dancing day and night."

—From a handbill, printed up to celebrate the first ascent (via a wooden ladder) of Devils Tower.

≍

"Greg, we gotta do this thing tomorrow. We're almost out of booze."

—**Jim Donini,** to Greg Crouch, beneath Mount Bradley on the Ruth Glacier.

≍

"There are all kinds of values to be gotten out of climbing. Sometimes you can take a girlfriend up a climb and get laid for it."

—**Steve Wunsch**

≍

"This new demonstration of your sincerity brings into higher relief the daring and sturdy characteristics one usually predicts of dedicated mountain climbers. Permit us to return herewith your check: it may be useful in forwarding your adventures and good luck with them."

—**Father Murphy's** letter, returning $12 to a Yosemite climber trying to repay the chapel after he had turned up the heating system and destroyed all the candles during his break-in and bivouac.

"I have *always* thought that heroism must be rarer at dawn than in the evening—I often observed the fact in Alpine huts: in the evening everyone is praying for fine weather the next day, and when the next day comes they wish that it was raining."

—René Dittert

≍

"Well, Collie, I've tasted cider back in old Michigan that beats this stuff all to hell."

—Packer Fred Stephens, on top of Mount Edith, complaining about Norman Collie's favorite champagne.

≍

"Expatriate rabble with their hair in leonine disarray."

—Jeff Long, describing Yosemite Valley climbers in his novel, *Angels of Light.*

≍

"Climbing is no longer the best thing to do in this area."

—Rick Sylvester's partner **Bernard,** commenting on the nude women suntanning on the beaches beneath the Calanques climbs.

≍

"At either end of the social spectrum there lies a leisure class."

—Eric Beck

"I've been sick on Beinn Alligin's summit,
I've puked on the slopes of Beinn Eigbe
And Slioch is crowned with my vomit
For such is the tribute I pay. . . .
But who is the keener I question,
The hardened athlete in his prime
Or the man with the failing digestion
Who conquers both it and his climb."

—**Douglas Fraser,** *Song of An Unfit Climber*

≍

"Soft, succulent people should go the mule way."

—**John Muir,** in reference to climbing the
Mountaineers Route on Mount Whitney, instead of
the standard route.

≍

"How is it Mac, that you can climb so well, when you are so
decadent?"

—An unidentified Russian to Ian McNaught-Davis,
smoking a cigarette atop 24,600-foot Peak
Communism.

"This fucking Pamir rock!"

—**Malcolm Slesser,** reaching the same summit
somewhat later.

COMMITMENT AND DESIRE

"Whatever you can do, or dream you can, begin it. Boldness has genius, power and magic in it."

    —**Goethe**

COMMITMENT AND DESIRE

Johann Wolfgang von Goethe was born in an era in which alpinism was only beginning to bud. But as a poet and lover of nature, he wrote about seeing Mont Blanc against the horizon and left inspirational words that spoke to the heart of climbers' sense of individuality. His "*magic*" quote rang its clarion call to climbers in a book, *Everest: The West Ridge*. Goethe's words ran below a W. H. Murray quote, in plain but unmistakable Times Roman typestyle; both quotes also appeared beneath a poster-photograph (by Barry Bishop) of two dot-sized climbers approaching the massive and unclimbed West Ridge. No committed climber could look at it without being inspired. Ten years later, Rick Ridgeway named his Everest book *The Boldest Dream*; numerous magazine articles carried the quote as an opening inspiration. By the 1990s, "dream . . . boldness" had even become somewhat saddle worn.

Yet, for climbers, Goethe's inspiration still endures. Because climbers dream of launching off onto that one great climb, something that initially seems beyond our grasp or ability, but will transform us once completed—as Willi Unsoeld and Tom Hornbein were transformed in 1963 by their bold ascent of the West Ridge. That initial commitment can seem so overwhelming that once you give yourself to it, the feeling is like being swept along in a riptide. Or as the renowned boulderer John Gill wrote about similar commitments, "My limbs became very light, my breathing altered very subtly, and I'm sure there were vascular changes that I wasn't really aware of at the time. . . . It was exhilarating and intense but almost in a relaxed way."

For me, this most committing of all climbs happened to be the Cassin Ridge of Denali (or McKinley) in winter of 1982, a cold journey that no one else, to my knowledge, had seriously contemplated, let alone attempted. I had imagined this climb for years. By mentally visualizing the sort of climbing movements as well as the wonder of a subzero spur of granite and ice above all of North America—by *dreaming* about it—I was able to prepare myself for the cold and desperate reality that followed. In retrospect, getting psyched was one part physical training and two parts mental preparation. Certainly, our commitment could be described as boldness because my partners and I exposed ourselves to some of the coldest conditions on earth during a technically challenging climb. I contracted pulmonary edema and frostbite; Mike Young was also frostbitten; Roger Mear tore ligaments in a bad crevasse fall.

I know now that it was nothing short of magic revealed in the fifty-below zero cloud undercast that occluded everything but ourselves on an island of ivory beauty and allowed us to finish our climb. It was indeed magic to find that the initial commitment and inner strength can bring you back down alive in the midst of such an undertaking.

▲ ▲ ▲

"Until one is committed there is hesitancy, the chance to draw back, always ineffectiveness. Concerning all acts of initiative (and creation) there is one elementary truth, the ignorance of which kills countless ideas and splendid plans: that the moment one definitely commits oneself, then Providence moves, too. All sorts of things occur to help one that would never otherwise have occurred. A whole stream of events issues from the decision, raising in one's favor all manner of unforeseen incidents and meetings and material assistance, which no man could have dreamt would have come his way."

—**W. H. Murray**

≍

"Something hidden—Go and find it! Go and look behind the Ranges

Something lost behind the Ranges, Lost and waiting for you. Go!"

—**Rudyard Kipling**

≍

"The climb will go. Get rid of the rope. It's only distracting you."

—**Jeff Lowe's** inner voice before committing to his
Bridal-veil Falls solo.

"I cannot imagine a sport other than climbing which offers such a complete and fulfilling expression of individuality. And I will not give it up nor even slow down, not for man, woman, nor wife, nor God."

    —**Chuck Pratt**

≍

"Eastward the dawn rose, ridge behind ridge into the morning, and vanished out of eyesight into guess; it was no more than a glimmer blending with the hem of the sky, but it spoke to them, out of memory and old tales, of the high and distant mountains."

    —**J. R. R. Tolkien**

≍

"Hi, this is Annie. I can't meet you this week because I'm off to Patagonia. I decided to go just today—I'll be in touch when I get back."

    —The outgoing phone message on **Annie Whitehouse's** machine.

≍

"The Cassin wasn't the ultimate, what it really did is open my mind to other possibilities."

    —**Mugs Stump,** after his 27½-hour solo of Denali in 1991.

"Indeed, whatever agonies and miseries the sufferer may endure on his pilgrimage to the heights, and however often he may swear never to return there, longing to do so is certain to recur."

—C. F. Meade

≍

"I have been constantly asked, with a covert sneer, 'Did it repay you?'—a question which involves the assumption that one wants to be repaid, as though the labor were not itself part of the pleasure."

—Sir Leslie Stephen

≍

"This is art? Climbing on zits. Switch fingers one at a time. Contrapuntal elegance. Left foot slides—up, now or never, and place it under the same side's fingers . . . in slow motion cartwheel upwards thinly . . . a vertical hold slips by . . . 'Got it!' Ape-like up on buckets."

—**Wayne Goss,** on the first free ascent of the Diamond.

≍

"If thy heart fails thee,
climb not at all."

—**Queen Elizabeth I**

"It is not the critic who counts, not the man who points out how the strong man stumbled or where the doer of deeds could have done them better. The credit belongs to the man who is actually in the arena; whose faith is marred by dust and sweat and blood; who strives valiantly; who errs and comes short again and again; who knows the great enthusiasms, the great devotions, and spends himself in a worthy cause; who, at the best, knows the triumph of high achievement; and who, at the worst, if he fails, at least fails while daring greatly, so that his place will never be with those cold and timid souls who know neither victory or defeat."

—**President Theodore Roosevelt,** who climbed the
     Matterhorn in 1881 and became an honorary
     member of the American Alpine Club in 1905.

≍

"Naked of life, naked of warmth and safety, bare to the sun and stars, beautiful in its stark snow loneliness, the Mountain waits."

—**Elizabeth Knowlton**

≍

"I see the usefulness of climbing not in the further development of technique, rather in the development of the instinct and proficiency of man to extend himself."

—**Reinhold Messner**

"I grew up exuberant in body but with a nervy, craving mind. It was wanting more, something tangible. It sought for reality intensely, always if it were not there. . . . But you see at once what I do. I climb."

> —**John Menlove Edwards**

≍

"What I feel very strongly now is that I've been looking for something completely new through these experiences. I feel myself like a 100-meter runner who is doing his best to cut just 0.1 second off the world record."

> —**Naomi Uemura,** preparing to make the first ever
> solo of Denali in 1970.

≍

"No pay, no prospects, not much pleasure."

> —**H. W. Tilman,** from an ad placed in the London
> *Times,* encouraging climbers to join him on long
> sailboat journeys to far-off peaks.

≍

"To venture causes anxiety, but not to venture is to lose one's self. . . . And to venture in the highest is precisely to become conscious of one's self."

> —**Søren Kierkegaard,** Danish philosopher,
> 1813–1855.

"I believe that no man can be completely able to summon all his strength, all his will, all his energy, for the last desperate move, till he is convinced the last bridge is down behind him and that there is nowhere to go but on."

—Heinrich Harrer

ACCIDENTS AND EPICS

[What about] those who drive in rush hour traffic or work a hundred hours a week? For experienced mountaineers, the odds of survival, if we look at the data carefully, are definitely better than for many other endeavors, especially if we meet the challenges with skill and experience."

—**Jed Williamson's** editorial in *Accidents in North American Mountaineering 1995*, answering a newspaper editor about why climbers defy the odds.

ACCIDENTS AND EPICS

The ultimate compendium of climber mishaps is contained in that annual publication, *Accidents in North American Mountaineering*. No one can be unaffected by this slim volume, whose luridly described downfalls sooner or later intersect our entire community. It is certainly the only climbing journal in the world that most practitioners and aspiring writers actually try to keep their names *out of.*

From 1973 to 1993, I became involved—professionally, inadvertently, and accidentally—in mountain rescue. For a few years, I wrote rescuer reports for that most ominous of all climbing journals.

I got involved in searching, rescuing, (self rescuing), and advising those climbers who might accept suggestions. I treated and dealt with those who got frostbitten, lost, benighted, stuck in a crevasse, stormbound, or injured. Death, however, was always a thing apart (see "The Great Divide"). Another epical failure that *is* included in this chapter, were those too-grand adventure victims who saw themselves as heroes.

As a rescuer, I never said no to helping an injured climber, and I probably developed some sort of predilection for carrying heavy weights on my back, performing first aid, and breathing bottled oxygen during thrilling helicopter rides through storm-buffeted mountains. It didn't hurt that I received hazard pay for many of those call-outs. Yet I couldn't help but notice that most of these so-called victims could have dealt with their own rescue, rather than putting rescuers or pilots at risk.

Even for those who are not in the rescue business, the odds are good that any active climber will eventually be called upon to perform samaritan acts. There are so many people out there that you can't help but run into a victim, or better yet, become one yourself. Every cragger, sportclimber, alpinist, or wallrat has had their own accident experience: descending a cliff with a dislocated shoulder, a lost partner, blown-away tents, hair stuck in a rappel, cut ropes, rockfall, hunger, long leader falls, or avalanches. Many of these epics are spiced up by an understatement that tells the whole story in a single sentence.

▲ ▲ ▲

"Henry . . . Headlamp."

—George Lowe's wife, **Liz Regan-Lowe,** revealing her
husband's middle name, then correcting herself as
she remembers how often he is caught out in the
dark.

≍

"Your poor judgment has caused a great halt in my personal
Xmas affairs; there are going to be a considerable number who
receive Xmas cards late on account of you."

—**Ed Roper's** letter to his son Steve, who spent
thirteen days in a hospital after falling 600 feet
during his unroped ice climb.

≍

"Are you all right?"

—**Hermann Buhl,** who had just taken a 200-foot
leader fall, yelled up to his partner.

"Yes! Are *you* alive?"

—The reply to Buhl.

"Each climber loses one finger or toe once in a while. This is a small but important reason for Polish climbers' success. Western climbers haven't lost as many fingers or toes."

—Wanda Rutkiewicz

≍

"Biscuit. I almost had it."

—The ever-reverent **Tobin Sorenson,** after narrowly missing a hand hold and slamming into a wall during a long leader fall.

≍

"I fell about twenty feet free and during that fall I saw all my friends and family in a large group. And I thought how stupid it was that I was falling and that I didn't want to die. That's when I saw the jammed haul rope come within reach and I knew I had a chance, albeit a slim one. I grabbed that rope— and still thought I was not going to make it because it burned my hands instantly. I slid on that rope for about thirty feet and then I stopped myself. I was hyperalert—I didn't believe that I could hold myself. It all happened so very fast. Somehow hanging on the rope by one hand, I managed to unclip from the useless rappel rope, clip into the haul rope that was still anchored back up at the belay, and rappel down to the top pitch off the Edge."

—**Coral Wilber,** riding the *Naked Edge* in Colorado.

"Frostbite? I consider that a failure."

—**Marc Twight,** never frostbitten after sixteen years of
mountaineering and ice climbing.

≍

"10 March . . . 0 hours climbing. Write five pages to my
mother-in-law. Getting desperate."

—**Dave Johnston's** journal, on sixth day stormbound
on Mount Foraker, Alaska.

≍

"My knuckles were so big in France that coins would fall
between my fingers."

—**Mike Freeman,** longtime hard rock man, after a
nine-month climbing trip.

≍

"When the slab cut loose, my mind calculated trajectories,
analyzed terrain, and fed me its conclusion—no way out—
you're going to die. This conclusion seemed to free me to experience the fall. Tumbling, catching air, then the loudest sound
I've ever heard—probably the reverberations of both legs
breaking or how to get hit with a Mack truck."

—**Carl Tobin,** on breaking his legs in the Alaska
Range.

"It is the momentary carelessness in easy places, the lapsed attention, or the wandering look that is the usual parent of disaster."

—**Albert F. Mummery**

≍

"I wouldn't mention this to my wife, ja?"

—**Richard Hechtel,** 57, after bouncing thirty feet
down, just missing the ground.

≍

"Then there was silence, hiss of the slide soft hushed.
The mountains lay, stood, reared like creatures that dream
lovely in sunlight: ebony, silver and silk
just as before. But I loathed them, trembling and sick,
for you had gone."

—**Wilfrid Noyce**

≍

"Don't fall now or we'll both go."

—**Layton Kor,** to a great number of partners over the
years, regarding the security of his routes.

≍

"The best part is getting to the top 'cause the pain's all over."

—**Dan Osman**

"Er, I say, are you going to be able to get me out?"

—**Eric Shipton's** voice emerging from a crevasse on a remote Patagonian glacier.

≍

"Some mountaineers are proud of having done all their climbs without bivouac. How much they have missed! And the same applies to those who enjoy only rock climbing, or only the ice climbs, only the ridges or the faces. We should refuse none of the thousand and one joys that the mountains offer us at every turn. We should brush nothing aside, set no restrictions. We should experience hunger and thirst, be able to go fast, but also know how to go slowly and to contemplate."

—**Gaston Rébuffat**

≍

"If you can stop five men at 25,000 feet, how many could you stop at 15,000?"

—**Bob Bates,** to Pete Schoening, immediately after his life-saving boot ax belay on K2.

≍

"Looks like we found the fast way down."

—**Rick White,** to his partners Doug Scott and Georges Bettemborg, after he and Greg Child fell 700 feet off the summit ridge of Shivling.

"Look out, Wiggerl."

>—**Andreas Heckmair,** before falling onto his partner
and cramponing his hand during their first ascent of
the Eiger's North Face.

≍

"It's a person's attitude toward life that is important, not
whether they're in a wheelchair or not."

>—**Mark Wellman,** who climbed El Cap and Half
Dome after being paralyzed in a climbing accident.

≍

"Pieces are coming off my bad ear."

>—From **John Edwards's** diary during the winter climb
of Denali, 1967.

≍

"Bedsores are the most likely injury on an expedition."

>—**Eric Shipton**

≍

"Do you think I'll make it?"

>—**Catherine Destivelle,** after suffering a compound
fracture of her leg on top of Mount Viets in
Antarctica.

"They catched are in an entangled net,
'Cause they good counsel lightly did forget:
'Tis true they rescued were; but yet, you see,
They're scourged to boot. Let this your caution be."

> **—John Bunyan**

≍

"Grand! What a lucky break for me. Now I can have another go next year!"

> **—Claudio Corti,** to Lionel Terray after he (Corti) lost his partner and was rescue-winched up the North Face of the Eiger.

≍

"The first blood."

> **—Mr. Hashimoto,** after being hit by rockfall during the first ascent of Mount Alberta in 1925, wiped his white gloves across his face and got a few laughs from his companions.

≍

"I'm not sensitive about my accidents, I'm sensitive about being [considered] a bad or foolish climber. Apart from the avalanche, and the ice climbing thing—those were my fault— the others were not my fault."

> **—Joe Simpson,** master of accident epics.

"Oh, it doesn't look so bad, Moll."

> —Anonymous "guy" to Molly Higgins, teeth bloodily buckled, after falling thirty feet while holding the climbing rope in her mouth.

≍

"I stared blankly at my fingertips. The ends were black and desiccated, hard to the touch."

> —**Ed Webster,** high on Mount Everest without oxygen.

≍

"My puffed and bloody knees, ripe from the night, softly exploded in crimson berries on my dirty trouserless legs."

> —**Ed Drummond,** after climbing Yosemite's Lost Arrow Chimney.

≍

"As my own life began to slip away, I was struck with an overwhelming sense of how wonderful it is to be alive."

> —**Art Davidson,** on Denali in winter.

≍

"A hero is no braver than an ordinary man, but he is brave five minutes longer."

> —**Ralph Waldo Emerson**

"There was a climber named Bridwell
On Grade I's he did well.
But on a Grade VI, he got into a fix
And rappelled to the talus and hid well."

　　—Eric Beck

≍

"Twenty *frozen fingers, twenty* frozen toes
Two blistered faces, frostbite on the nose
One looks like Herzog, who dropped his gloves on top
And Lachenal tripped and fell, thought he'd never stop.
Bop bop bop bop bop bop bop bop bop.
'Take me down to Oudot' was all that he would say
'He'll know what to do now,' said Lionel Terray
'Your blood is like black pudding' said Oudot, with his knife
'It is not too late to amputate if I can save your life.'
Chop chop chop chop chop chop chop chop chop.
No tiny fingers, no tiny toes
The memory lingers but the digit goes
On an Eastern Railway carriage, where the River Ganges flows
There are Twenty Tiny Fingers and Twenty Tiny Toes.
Chop chop chop chop chop chop chop chop chop."

　　—Tom Patey's song about Maurice Herzog getting
　　frostbitten on Annapurna.

"I've had bullets go by within inches of my head but this was closer!"

> —**Jeff Hollenbaugh,** after running and ducking into a crevasse to avoid being hit by an avalanche on Mount St. Elias in 1995.

≍

"The biscuit was tough, and its frozen exterior yielded but little to my efforts. Suddenly it gave way and the knife broke through, cutting a deep gash in the palm of my left hand nearly two inches long. The wound was so deep that a number of the sensory nerves in the two little fingers were severed. I sat and watched the thick drops of blood ooze out and drip slowly onto my sleeping bag. Suddenly the significance of what had happened penetrated my altitude-benumbed consciousness."

> —**Arthur Emmons,** writing about being deprived from ascending Minya Konka.

≍

"No, we got here first. The Germans are ours."

> —**Gary Hemming,** to a French guide who was attempting to rescue the victims Hemming reached first on the West Face of the Petite Dru.

"Something was wrong. I couldn't put my finger on it, but something was definitely wrong. Suddenly I knew what it was. In the darkness, in the wind and in the confusion, I had come unclipped from the rappel line. Just as I realized it, it was already too late. The weight of the pack and the steepness of the wall made it impossible for me to keep my balance. With a despairing cry I pitched over backwards into the night sky."

> —**Duane Raleigh**

≍

"The game's up; we've got to go down!"

> —**Belmore Browne,** yelling to Herschel Parker during a storm that prevented them from climbing Denali's last 200 feet in 1912.

≍

"Men's resources of energy in the face of death are inexhaustible. When the end seems imminent, there still remain reserves, though it needs tremendous willpower to call them up."

> —**Maurice Herzog**

≍

"Welcome to Yosemite."

> —Rescuer **Yvon Chouinard's** first words to victim Jim McCarthy, who had broken his arm during a fall on El Capitan.

THE GREATEST HILL
ON EARTH

"I soon learned Everest was not a private affair. It belonged to many men."

　　　—Thomas Hornbein, after his ascent of the West Ridge.

THE GREATEST HILL ON EARTH

Among the cognoscenti of alpinism, climbing Mount Everest by its normal South Col route while using bottled oxygen is a mere collector climb. The tallest mountain in the world is certainly not the most difficult, and it is now accessible to any client willing to pay $65,000 in the hopes that the weather will allow guides and Sherpas to fix ropes, break trail, and lead clients to the top. The lay public will acknowledge a conquest of Everest's "Yak Route" to the exclusion of more difficult climbs—Yosemite walls, Alaskan peaks, Andean ice faces, even other Himalayan ascents. Climbing Everest by the South Col is also a sure invitation to lecture on the black-tie circuit, and after the media fascination with the eight deaths on the South Col Route in 1996, writers Jon Krakauer, Sandy Hill, and Anatoli Boukreev (killed in 1997) became household names.

So why include a chapter on Everest? Aside from the fact that the mountain has become a mainstream icon and a purplish metaphor for ennui-filled executives, the subcultural literature of climbing has always been flush with Everest references. It all began in 1852 with the apocryphal quote about the underling surveyor rushing up to Sir Andrew Waugh (the Surveyor General) and blurting out, "Sir! I have discovered the highest mountain in the world!"

A century later, after fifteen men died during a score of international attempts (mostly British), the New Zealander Ed Hillary and his Sherpa partner, Tenzing Norgay, became the first to summit after climbing the South Col route with bottled oxygen. Americans repeated the mountain thirteen years later, again with bottled oxygen, but by a daring new route on the challenging West Ridge (see Hornbein quote on preceding page). Other difficult new routes were climbed, such as the British and American invasions on the Southwest and East Faces, a notable lightweight and oxygen-bottle-free ascent of the demanding Kangshung Face, and two landmark climbs both orchestrated by Reinhold Messner. In 1978 he and Peter Habeler climbed the South Col Route without oxygen, and in 1980, Messner soloed the North Ridge without oxygen. Messner thereby became the most influential climber in history, changing the way alpinists (but not the general public or climbing clientele) thought about Everest, opening up the highest peaks in the world to being climbed without Sherpas and bottled oxygen and fixed ropes and stocked camps.

So Everest has accounted for a body of literature and history richer than that of any other climb or mountain in the world. Yet aside from the brief Coronation event that followed the first ascent, none of the truly significant climbs of Everest resulted in best-selling books or enduring media events. After all, who can relate to the genetic mutant, Messner, or the distant New Zealander, Hillary? But when the death toll mounted in 1996, the media latched onto the disaster, rather than the more historic and significant accomplishments.

One of the 1996 Everest guides, Anatoli Boukreev, complained after the tragedy, "How could the adventure seeker of today find satisfaction with a level of performance that was a standard set more than forty years ago?"

▲ ▲ ▲

"You're not going to be famous unless we get down alive."

—**Ed Webster,** to the exhausted Stephen Venables, descending the Kangshung Face after reaching the summit without oxygen.

≍

"Been there, done that."

—**Greg Child's** concluding sentence in his *Climbing* magazine story about reaching the summit via the North Ridge.

≍

"Sometime this mountain will also be climbed alone and with simple means."

—**Earl Denman,** who attempted a solo in 1947.

≍

"The highest mountain in the world, the ultimate mountaineering trophy, has become accessible to sort of ordinary Walter Mitty types with a spare 65,000 bucks."

—**Jon Krakauer**

"The problem is there is nowhere to go. And folk do need to go to the toilet on the way up and down."

> —**Kenneth Stewart,** with the British Everest Medical Expedition, suggesting the installation of a public lavatory to alleviate the unpleasant odors.

≍

"Well, we knocked the bastard off."

> —**Sir Edmund Hillary,** descending in 1950.

≍

"*The Conquest of Everest*"

> —The 1955 North American edition's renaming of John Hunt's *The Ascent of Everest.*

≍

"You are a daredevil. You never care for your home. What will happen to me and the children?"

> —**Mrs. Tenzing Botia,** Sherpa Tenzing's wife, on his seventh return to the mountain.

"I would rather die on Everest than in your hut."

> —**Sherpa Tenzing's** reply.

"Altitude is the great equalizer."

—Anonymous maxim cited by Everest climbers.

≍

"My primary concern is that Scott's kids and family feel good about what we did. I can only hope they feel that it wasn't too intrusive, and that it is something that contributes to their dealing with grief as opposed to contributing to their grief."

—**Peter Horton,** who played Scott Fischer in the ABC television movie ("Into Thin Air: Death on Everest") about the 1996 tragedy.

≍

"It seems kinda strange that Glenn didn't want me to talk about the rescue or Lhotse."

—**Scott Fischer,** on being usurped by the American Alpine Club President's South Col lecture at the 1990 annual meeting; Fischer had performed a rescue on that trip and made the more difficult ascent of neighboring Lhotse.

≍

"And today I know that the path between tomb and towering heights is extremely narrow."

—**Reinhold Messner,** after he and Peter Habeler first climbed Everest without oxygen.

"Naturally some of your brain cells have been destroyed, particularly those that are connected with your memory of places and people."

—**Dr. Oswald Ölz**, to Habeler and Messner after they climbed Everest without oxygen.

≍

"It stands to reason that men with any zest for mountaineering could not possibly allow Mount Everest to remain untouched. The time, the opportunity, the money, the ability to make the necessary preliminary preparation might be lacking, but the wish and the will to stand on the summit of the world's highest mountain must have been in the heart of many a mountaineer."

—**Sir Francis Younghusband**

≍

"I can't understand why men make all this fuss about Everest—it's only a mountain."

—**Junko Tabei**, first woman to climb it.

≍

"Reaching that windswept perch, I decided, would cleanse my spirit and heal my wounds. More than that, it would send me home with a title: The First American Woman to Climb Everest."

—**Stacy Allison**

"If the climbing of Everest is, as we have been told, an important stage in the victory of mind over matter, then let every conceivable method be adopted to ensure success. Let dynamite be taken to excavate a better platform for the tents at the highest camps; let the climbers be in sufficient numbers to be always at hand to help an exhausted man; let pitons be taken, cables fixed, and oxygen dumped at various points. It is by these mechanical inventions that the superstitious terrors of the natives will be destroyed, far more than by any sacrifice of life or health. And let everything possible be done to facilitate the ascent of future parties; otherwise there will be an appearance of withholding from others the benefits that an ascent of Everest confers."

—**R. L. G. Irving**

≍

"Lots of fucking beautiful postcards [scenes], but no fucking climbing."

> —**Jean Afanassieff**, trying to film Erhardt Loretan and Jean Troillet climbing the Super Direct, which they only climbed at night.

"The most exacting mountaineering that has ever been done in the Himalayas."

> —**General Bruce,** on Hermann Buhl's little-known solo of Nanga Parbat in 1953, just after Everest had first been climbed.

≍

"In mountaineering and exploration, efficiency does not depend on the amassing of material and manpower, so much as the power to improvise plans at a moment's notice. In a word, to be adaptable. It is the opportunist who is most successful in the Himalayas."

> —**Frank S. Smythe**

≍

"I had climbed my mountain, but I must still live my life."

> —**Tenzing Norgay**

≍

"One of my greatest regrets was going to Everest instead of going to Nanda Devi."

> —**Eric Shipton,** referring to the 1936 climb of the elegant peak in India

"Wouldn't Mallory be pleased if he knew about this?"

—**Sir Edmund Hillary,** descending.

≍

"We have founded a support group for Everest climbers called 'Everest Anonymous.' Members can call each other up for support when they're thinking about returning to the mountain."

—**David Breashears,** broadcasting by satellite from base camp to Colorado.

≍

"There is no essay on Mount Everest."

—From **James Ramsey Ullman's** *New York Times* book review of a mountaineering anthology published in 1950.

≍

"It is my destiny!"

—**John Petroske,** Everest climber, explaining his interest in riding a barrel down off the summit.

≍

"Everest is a matter of universal human endeavor, a cause from which there is no withdrawal, whatever losses it may demand."

—**G. O. Dyrenfurth**-1886–1905, German mountaineer and scholar.

"For a mountaineer, surely a Bonnington Everest Expedition is one of the last great Imperial experiences life can offer."

> —**Peter Boardman,** youngest climber on the 1975 siege style expedition.

≍

"I must make top, you know. I no want go up more but, is not possible to make sponsors if no success here."

> —**Marc Batard,** trying to reach the summit in twenty-four hours.

≍

"We encourage young people to go out and exceed their goals. Everest is an icon of that."

> —**Neil Beidleman,** quoted by a newspaper reporter after the 1996 tragedy.

≍

"It is an amiable illusion, which the shape of our planet prompts, that every man is at the top of the world."

> —**Ralph Waldo Emerson**

≍

"I have not had to buy lunch since."

> —**Stephen Venables,** when asked how climbing Everest has changed his life.

FAMOUS CLIMBS

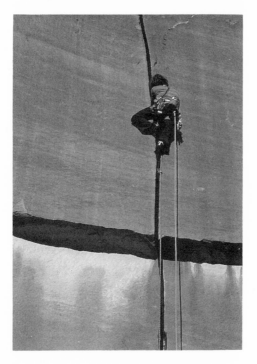

"Climbers seem to forget that we said in our introduction that these were simply '50 classic climbs,' not '*the* 50 classics.' We chose 50 from a list of about 120. Only a torturer will ever pry loose from our lips the names of those other 70 classics. . . . Thank God we opted for a full treatment of 50, rather than a cursory treatment of all 120."

> —**Steve Roper,** on his and Allen Steck's famous book, *Fifty Classic Climbs of North America.*

FAMOUS CLIMBS

Climbing is one of the few sports in which the arena—the cliffs, the mountains, and their specific routes—acquire a notoriety that outpopulates, outshines, and outlives the actual athletes. In other sports it is the athletes (rather than the arena) whom you think of first: Babe Ruth, Joe Namath, Jack Nicklaus, Arthur Ashe, or Billy Kidd. Mention famed climbers Lynn Hill, John Roskelley, Fritz Wiessner, Fred Beckey, or Royal Robbins and most people won't know who they all are. Mention the climbing arenas, however, such as the Eiger, El Capitan, Cerro Torre, Joshua Tree, McKinley, Devils Tower, City of Rocks, K2, Valdez, Everest, or the Gunks and even the uninitiated will bob their heads in recognition.

Some climbs—such as the North Face of the Eiger and K2's Abruzzi Ridge—become famous because of fatalities; more than one mountain range (such as Patagonia) is famous because of equipment companies; and fifty particular climbs in North America are famous, at least in climbers' eyes, because of a book called *Fifty Classic Climbs of North America*. "The Book," as it's known to many climbers, is an offbeat amalgam of history, pure-looking routes, and inadvertently, dangerous routes. For example, it took two decades for The Book's Hummingbird Ridge on Mount Logan (death toll: two) to be repeated, and seven decades for Abruzzi Ridge on Mount St. Elias (death toll: four) to be repeated.

Fifty Classic Climbs authors, Allen Steck and Steve Roper, followed on the heels of similar European best-sellers known as the "Rébuffat series," which included such books as "The 100 Finest Routes of Mont Blanc." *Fifty Classics* (hardly fifty *famous*) became a subcult hit in the U.S. The Book has sold nearly thirty thousand copies in the two decades since it was first published, which, by climbing guidebook standards, is an exceptional sales record.

Most of the climbs listed (with the exception of a half dozen awe-inspiring routes in Canada and Alaska that are rarely repeated) have become increasingly popular since The Book was first published in 1979. Its publisher, the Sierra Club, is no doubt sorry for whatever indirect environmental degradation The Book has caused to these fifty wilderness destinations. The park rangers on Denali recently staged a cleanup climb on the Cassin Ridge (included in The Book), pulling off hundreds of pounds of garbage. Nor is it uncommon to line up and wait your turn beneath such former sleepers as The Book's Petite Grepon, the Ellingwood Arête, the Nose, Castleton Tower, or Stuart's North Ridge. And now a plethora of other "classic" facsimile books have inundated climbing stores.

Still, there is no being who has actually completed all one hundred of the "finest routes," let alone the "fifty classics"—but many climbers talk about it. If and when these feats are actualized, the ascensionists, for a short period of time, will actually become more famous than the arenas.

▲ ▲ ▲

"God made the mountains, but good God! who made Robson?"

—**Conrad Kain,** first ascensionist of the Kain Face.

≍

"It's the hardest climb I've ever done."

—**Fred Beckey,** discussing Devils Thumb.

≍

"The climb waits for someone with stainless steel testicles."

—**Roger Briggs,** on who would complete the free ascent of Colorado's Jules Verne in 1975.

"When we got to the top I was gonna ask Steve to pull down his pants."

—**Steve Erickson** commenting about Steve Wunsch's freeing Jules Verne in 1977.

≍

"For those who appreciate the weird contortions of Acrobatic Alpinism."

—The Colorado Mountain Club journal editor on Albert Ellingwood's 1929 climb of Crestone Needle.

"Charlie, if you ever want to see Dorcas and Penny again, climb up there *right now!*"

> —**Bob Bates,** after a bad fall on the Abruzzi Ridge of
> K2 in 1953, reminding the concussed Charles
> Houston of his wife and daughter.

≍

"New things are done by simply trying them again and again and again until one succeeds."

> —**John Stannard,** on introducing 5.11 to the east coast
> with Foops (at the Gunks).

≍

"It is a crest of granite. . . . perfectly inaccessible, being probably the only one of all the prominent points about the Yosemite which never has been, and never will be, trodden by human foot."

> —The 1865 report of the California Geological Survey
> on Half Dome.

≍

"Never claim a first ascent in North America because Beckey probably did it first."

> —Anonymous aphorism.

"The falling rocks, they are one of the many natural hazards climbers must face in the Alps. If you do not like the climbing here, perhaps you should return to America, where the mountains are not so big."

—A French climber to Jon Krakauer, who complained to the Frenchman and his partner about knocking rocks down on him while climbing the North Face of the Tour Ronde.

≍

"One thing to remember on the Eiger, never look up, or you may need a plastic surgeon."

—Don Whillans

≍

"Hell, I wasn't worried about those guys. I figured they'd get out. It was just a matter of *when*, rather than *whether*."

—Bush pilot **Bob Reeves,** after abandoning Bradford Washburn and Bob Bates to a 125-mile walkout, which forced the climbers to initiate the unclimbed traverse of Lucania and Steele.

≍

"Step on the piton!"

—Fritiof Fryxell, coaching his partner during the first ascent of the North Face of the Grand Teton.

"Guido, the sardine tin!"

> —**Lionel Terray,** to Guido Magnone on the summit
> headwall of Fitzroy in 1952, after realizing their last
> piton had been used as an opener and left with the
> sardine can inside his pack.

≍

"I continued with whatever 'qualified climbers' I could con
into this rather unpromising venture."

> —**Warren Harding,** on the first ascent of El Capitan's
> Nose Route.

≍

"If you don't do it, that bastard Washburn will be back next
year."

> —**Andy Taylor,** to Allen Carpé and Terris Moore
> several thousand feet below the unclimbed summit
> of Mount Fairweather.

≍

"We climb only for sport."

> —**The Duke of Abruzzi,** to a reporter trying to
> understand his motivations for going to Mount St.
> Elias in 1897.

"I felt part of some great movement, one of an infinite scale, too grand to see but only to feel in the night's wind."

—**Mugs Stump,** bivouacking on the North Buttress of Mount Hunter, 1981.

≍

"Even if we were successful, there would be no crowds of hero worshippers, no newspaper reports. Thank goodness American climbing has not yet progressed to that sorry state."

—**Yvon Chouinard,** on the first ascent of Yosemite's Muir Wall, 1966.

≍

"The climbing was pretty stiff, I must say, though not nearly so difficult as the Grépon, which is a real snorker."

—**Lily Bristow,** on the Dru before the turn of the century.

≍

"Mont Blanc is the monarch of mountains
They crowned him long ago
On a throne of rocks, in a robe of clouds,
With a diadem of snow."

—**Lord Byron**

"I send my warmest congratulations to you and to the other members of the Italian team, who have achieved such a splendid mountaineering feat on Mt. McKinley."

> —**President John F. Kennedy,** to Riccardo Cassin in 1961.

≍

"If mankind doesn't kill himself first—on a mountain or with a bomb—he just may learn how to inhabit the earth as God planned."

> —*San Francisco News* editorial after the first ascent of El Capitan's Nose.

SUMMITS

"I'm glad we left no footmark on the top."

> —**George Bond,** on the first ascent of Kanchenjunga's sacred summit.

SUMMITS

I have had the privilege of climbing on peaks where no one had ever stood before. One beautiful and now sought after peak in the Garwhal Himalayas, Thelay Sagar, was the experience of a lifetime. But it wasn't the actual climb—which was nasty for its rock- and icefall, our small Anglo-American team's divisiveness, and my sickness—that remains with me. It was the cultural aspect that enlightened me: the villagers who had never seen Westerners, sharing an ashram with monks below the peak, and the fanatical-eyed look of the pilgrims journeying to their sacred headwaters in stark mimicry of our team's obsessiveness with Thelay Sagar. Even if I *had* made the last 2,000 feet to the summit, the dizzying cultural encounters would still have subsumed the climb. A photograph of our climb appeared on a 1980 cover of *Climbing* magazine; all four of us published stories.

Years later, on an unclimbed Alaskan mountain named Triple Crown, my three Alaskan friends and I got on splendidly, none of us got sick, and we climbed with a spontaneity and drive that downplayed the rotten shale and hanging glacier reputation of the peak. We boldly stomped out to the eave of the summit cornice on tight ropes, ate a long and casual lunch, and grew dizzy with the glacier plunging into the mists a mile below. It took several blistering days of tussock walking and bushwhacking to reach the nearest dirt road.

We never published any accounts (until now) or photographs of our first ascent of Triple Crown—even though my three companions were known climbers and photographers. Yet Triple Crown remains one of my finest climbs because of the feeling of completion. And because we were all on a quest for natural beauty. It was the curve of the summit ridge's cornice. Our starry bivouacs. Then finally, being awoken one warm dawn by Dave Johnston's gasps of wonder, as he wandered buck naked and barefoot across a dense, flower-studded meadow, which we had unknowingly arrived at in the dark and bedded down in like four migrating caribou. This "feeling of completion" had little to do with reaching the summit—it was really about friendship, challenge, and our respect for the mountain environment.

I have passed through the area several times since, and gazed up at Triple Crown with great nostalgia, as though that quiet experience was all that climbing should ever aspire to. My last time in the Alaska Range, I sought to take these notions of respect and completion one step further. I wanted to apply Robert Pirsig's motto from *Zen and the Art of Motorcycle Maintenance:* "To live for some future goal is shallow. It is the sides of the mountains which sustain life, not the top."

So my companions and I traversed Denali from north to south, utilizing dogsleds, skiing a steep couloir alongside Triple Crown, then paddling back into civilization in kayaks—while filming it all for television. The trip was successful largely because of the selflessness of the climbers I accompanied. No one got injured, we all became friends, and we even got our film footage from the summit. It was altogether unprecedented: putting all that beautiful film footage "in the can," seventeen continuous days of sunshine among the thirty-six-day outing, and the cooperative spirit of our climb.

On the summit, I had sprung a surprise while standing just below the top, refusing to make the last few steps. I explained why to the cameraman: "Our trip is not about making the top, it's about something greater, and by stopping below the summit, this is my gesture of respect to the mountain."

"One sees great things from the valley;
only small things from the peak."

 —**G. K. Chesterton,** British essayist, 1874–1936.

≍

"I also know that by denying ourselves the summit, we denied ourselves the very special feeling that makes alpine climbing the exceptional sport it is."

 —**Jack Roberts,** on the North Face of Mount Kennedy.

≍

"Where's the Branch Bank?"

 —**Peter Boardman,** reciting the lines for a sponsor's commercial into a tape recorder while standing on the summit of Everest.

≍

"It's a round trip. Getting to the summit is optional, getting down is mandatory."

 —**Ed Viesturs**

"I felt curiously unsteady, drunk almost, but not with exultation. It was rather a feeling of finality, conclusiveness, but not of victory."

> —**Charles Houston,** on his first ascent of Mount
> Foraker, 1934.

≍

"Summit or death, either way, I win."

> —**Rob Slater,** before leaving for K2. He lost his life
> there.

≍

"Slight and tapering in form—though many of these needle-like peaks of Mont Blanc are, there is yet something calm and enduring in them. Such tremendous masonry as theirs will endure through countless generations, and when the noblest memorials of man have crumbled into dust and the twentieth century is but a faint mist on the backward horizon of eternity, these peaks will lift their proud summits into the clouds."

—Frank S. Smythe

≍

"It's good to have an end to journey toward; but it is the journey that matters, in the end."

—Ursula K. Le Guin

"I was pent up. I sure grabbed that girl of mine."

> —**Warren Harding,** on reaching the summit of El
> Capitan via the Nose in 1958.

≍

"We know you're up here somewhere. Don't play games with us. You can't fool us."

> —**Chuck Kroger,** on reaching the deserted summit of
> El Capitan's Heart Route in 1970, mimicking earlier
> pampered Yosemite summiteers.

≍

"After all these years of waiting, this is my gold medal."

> —**Jean Ellis,** first African-American to summit an
> 8,000-meter peak, Cho Oyu. He qualified for the
> Olympic marathon team in 1980, when the U.S.
> boycotted Moscow.

≍

"I believe that the ascent of mountains forms an essential chapter in the complete duty of man, and that it is wrong to leave any district without setting foot on its highest peak."

—Sir Leslie Stephen

"I was the first human being since Creation's Day to get there. But I felt no wave of overmastering joy, no wish to shout aloud, no sense of victorious exaltation."

> —**Hermann Buhl,** after soloing for seventeen hours to summit Nanga Parbat in 1953.

≍

"Is it the summit, crowning the day? How cool and quiet! We're not exultant; but delighted, joyful; soberly astonished . . . Have we vanquished an enemy? None but ourselves. Have we gained success? That word means nothing here."

> —**George Leigh Mallory**

≍

"I had reached the end of my journey, I had come to a place where no one—where neither the eagle nor the chamois had ever been before me. I had got there alone, without other help than that of my own will. Everything that surrounded me seemed to be my own property. I was the King of Mont Blanc—the statue of this tremendous pedestal."

> —**Jacques Balmat's** impressions on reaching the summit of Mont Blanc, 1786.

"In every landscape, the point of astonishment is the meeting of the sky and earth, and that is seen from the first hillock as well as from the top of the Alleghenies."

—**Ralph Waldo Emerson**

≍

"That was the Cervin, and I had been up it. And then, I must confess, that at bottom I felt almost sorry. I had many times dreamed of this ascent, which every climber is covetous to make. For a long time I had ardently hankered after this exploit, and now I was appeased. What a singular being is man, who burns to possess and, in the moment of possession, repents of his desire!"

—**Emile Javelle**

≍

"I love you baby, I'm on the summit."

—**Ray Genet's** opening salutation to three separate women during his three radio-phone calls from the summit of Denali in July 1976.

≍

"Covered with two feet of icy, windblown snow crystals—a spot just large enough so that one man could stand upon it."

—**Fritz Wiessner**, describing the top of Waddington in 1936.

"In order to see much one must learn to look away from oneself—every mountain climber needs this hardness. You must climb above yourself—up and beyond—until you have even your stars under you! Yes! To look down upon myself and even upon my stars: that alone would I call my summit, that has remained for me as my ultimate summit!"

—**Friedrich Nietzsche**

≍

"Gentlemen, that's as far as I can take you."

—**Conrad Kain,** to his clients, William Foster and
Albert MacCarthy, atop Robson in 1913.

≍

"We've come this far. Let's make the last step together."

—**Jim Wickwire,** to Lou Reichardt, putting their arms
around one another and becoming the first
Americans to reach the summit of K2 in 1978.

GETTING GRIPPED

"Come on, sir, here's the place: stand still. How fearful and dizzy 'tis to cast one's eyes so low."

    —**William Shakespeare**

GETTING GRIPPED

At the time of my first ice-climbing lead up a subzero New Hampshire gully, I had a race-car driver's photograph and quote on my bedroom wall that read "If you're scared you'll never drive again." But during that first climb, I fouled my pants in fear. Then safely back home I contemplated the poster's meaning and quickly planned my next climb.

On a large Alaskan climb, where it seemed that any number of acts of God (avalanches, storms, rockfall, cold, or falling) could off me with all the impunity of a slapped flea, I began praying for my life.

While caught in a hissing Colorado wet-slab avalanche, the adrenaline of fear electrified me into a contorted combination of butterfly stroke and leg sprinting until I burst out of the far side like a cork from a champagne bottle.

In Vermont, I walked up to the base of the dead-vertical ice hose that I wanted to climb and was so fearful of falling off that I simply turned around, walked back to my car, drove away, and never came back again.

All of these experiences held one thing in common: the process of fear ultimately seemed to preserve life and limb. Fear in the wrong place, of course, could have devastating consequences: letting your legs "Elvis" fifty feet above the last protection, delaying a summit bid during a brief weather window, or letting your partner know that you're scared when your perceived confidence was the only thing that was keeping him together.

There is a lot of jive talk propagated about fear, how we conquer it by climbing big rocks and elevated mountains, and how the real climbing hero can never afford to be scared. And it's all malarkey, just like the race car driver quote of my youth. It is surprising that many climbers rarely write or talk about being scared (consequently, some of the following quotes are gleaned from those outside of the game), as if acknowledging one's fear would end one's vertical career. But if the fear is always inside of us, perhaps we need to accept it.

▲　▲　▲

"The reason it was so scary was that there was only one climber capable of rescuing us, and that was Layton Kor, and he was in Colorado."

> —**Yvon Chouinard,** writing about the first ascent of the North American Wall in 1964.

≍

"Never again."

> —**Mrs. Hettie Dyrenfurth,** after climbing Queen Maud Peak (24,000 feet) in the Baltoro (the women's high altitude record that she held onto for twenty years).

≍

"The moment of terror is the beginning of life, Mike, so take the 'No Fear' stickers off your truck."

> —**Marc Twight,** in reply to a question about whether his angst was for real or just a promotional ploy.

≍

"Fain would I climb, yet fear I to fall."

> —**Sir Walter Raleigh,** 1552–1618, English explorer and writer.

"Oh, this climbing, that involves an effort, on every move the holds to be spotted and often there are none, then every limb placed, the body set into the one suitable position found but with trouble, then with the whole organism great force must be exerted, before anything happens, and this is to be done while the brain is occupied sick and stiff with its fears: and now you have been doing this for well over an hour and a half and the strain must be telling: get down therefore."

—**John Menlove Edwards**

≍

"It is not a good thing to look at great walls for too long a time."

—**Yvon Chouinard,** after waiting for days to try the enormous, snow-plastered north face of Mount Edith Cavell.

≍

"Now I don't worry about falling but I'm no different from any of those women: I'm not bold, I'm not brave; in fact, I'm a total chickenshit."

—**Shelley Presson**

"First, he should never show fear. Second, he should be courteous to all, and always give special attention to the weakest member in the party. Third, he should be witty, and able to make up a white lie if necessary, on short notice, and tell it in a convincing manner. Fourth, he should know when and how to show authority . . . and should be able to give a good scolding to whomsoever deserves it."

—**Conrad Kain,** on being a companionable guide.

≍

"I'm happy to be here because this is the last time I will ever be on a desert tower."

—**Megan Currier's** note in a summit register,
Independence Monument, Colorado.

≍

"At first, I was so affected by the unaccustomed spirit of the air, and by the free prospect, that I stood as one stupefied."

—**Petrarch,** the Italian poet and scholar, on Mount
Ventoux.

≍

"A good scare is worth more to a man than good advice."

—**Ed Howe,** American journalist and author.

"He pressed on, turning right and left among rocky, snow-clad elevations, and came behind them on an incline, then a level spot, then on the mountains themselves—how alluring and accessible seemed their softly covered gorges and defiles! His blood leaped at the strong allurement of the distance and the height, the ever profounder solitude. At risk of a late return he pressed on, deeper into the wild silence, the monstrous and the menacing, despite that gathering darkness was sinking down over the region like a veil, and heightening his inner apprehension until it presently passed into actual fear."

    —**Friedrich Nietzsche**

≍

"I was quaking in my boots."

    —**Lynn Hill**, after dropping a crucial stopper on the
       crux pitch during her free ascent of El Capitan's
       Nose in a day.

≍

"People who are afraid of heights need to work at this problem step by step, day by day, climb by climb."

    —**Zoe Bundros**

"And now I found these fancies creating their own realities, and all imagined horrors crowding upon me in fact. I felt my knees strike violently together, while my fingers were gradually but certainly relaxing their grasp. And now I was consumed with the irrepressible desire of looking below. I could not, I would not, confine my glances to the cliff; and, with a wild, indefinable emotion, half of horror, half of a relieved oppression, I threw my vision far down into the abyss. For one moment my fingers clutched convulsively upon their hold, while, with the movement, the faintest possible idea of ultimate escape wandered, like a shadow, through my mind—in the next my whole soul was pervaded with a longing to fall."

—**Edgar Allan Poe,** bard of the macabre, 1809–1849.

≍

"An essential difference is that the mountaineer usually accepts the challenge on his own terms, whereas once at sea, the sailor has no say in the matter and in consequence may suffer more often the salutary and humbling emotion of fear."

—**H. W. Tilman,** comparing climbing to sailing.

≍

"I wouldn't use fear as the word to characterize the way I normally feel when I climb Everest."

—**David Breashears**

"Climb higher and gaze into the distance,
Your heart will be gripped with fear.
Cirques of chasms surrounded by peaks,
Frowning cliffs all around;
Loose rocks that lean over the abyss,
escarpments that overhang each other
Clinging like a climbing bear,
you remain frozen in place,
Perspiration dripping down to your feet.
You feel yourself lost, reeling,
Transfixed with anguish, out of yourself;
And your spirit, shaken loose,
plunges into terrors without cause.

—**Sung Yü,** Chinese poet, fourth century B.C.

≍

"No, we are neither hard nor foolhardy; we shall never be so.
We are miserable, fearful rabbits who overcome our fear,
sometimes with a surge of courage if it is really necessary. *Son
of Heart* was for me a trip into an unexplored country, the land
of my own psyche. I had never thought that I could muster so
much faith in myself after so much anxiety and despondency."

—**Reinhard Karl** on El Capitan (died in an avalanche
on Cho Oyu in 1982).

"In order to climb properly on a big peak one must free one-self of fear. This means you must write yourself off before any big climb. You must say to yourself, 'I may die here.'"

> —**Doug Scott**

≍

"I'm afraid to be afraid."

> —**Catherine Destivelle**

≍

"I'm finished."

> —**Hermann Buhl,** slumping down on his belay stance after leading the crux pitch on the North Face of the Eiger.

≍

"A queasy feeling hit my stomach. Steep walls and fluted ridges rose up at unbelievable angles in numerous thousand-foot sweeps. All were plastered by huge hanging glaciers, menacing cornices and weird snow formations."

> —**Peter Metcalf,** getting his first glimpse of the Reality Ridge route on Denali.

≍

"I banish fear, you lead."

> —Bumper sticker.

"We promise according to our hopes,
and perform according to our fears."

> —**François de La Rochefoucauld**, seventeenth-century
> French epigrammatist.

≍

"For it is the ultimate wisdom of the mountains that man is
never so much a man as when he is striving for what is beyond
his grasp, and that there is no battle worth winning save that
against his own ignorance and fear."

> —**James Ramsey Ullman**

≍

"Fear is one of the countless sensations felt by the climber and
which, combined with others, gives him the reason for his
existence. Beware if you do not experience fear in the mountains. Not to do so would mean that one was devoid of feeling
and no longer able to experience the supreme joy of knowing
that one has mastered fear. Mountaineering can, indeed, be
more dangerous than any other human activity, but if one
comes to the mountains carefully prepared and observes rea-
sonable prudence, it becomes something far different from
mere foolish recklessness."

> —**Walter Bonatti**

"The restfulness and the utter silence reigning in the vast spaces spread out before my eyes, which imagination pictured vaster still, inspired in me a feeling akin to terror: I seemed to be the sole Survivor of the Universe, and that was its corpse I saw stretched beneath my feet."

—**Horace Bénédict de Saussure,** Swiss scientist
   attempting Mont Blanc in 1785.

≍

"At risk of a late return he pressed on, deeper into the wild silence, the monstrous and the menacing, despite that gathering darkness was sinking down over the region like a veil, and heightening his inner apprehension until it presently passed into actual fear."

—From **Thomas Mann's** novel *The Magic Mountain*,
   about Castorp climbing into a snowstorm.

HUBRIS

"How unrefreshing is the insight that, like the ego itself, climbing in its outer sense is an abstraction that has become obsessed with its own image and needs continual reassertion in the mirrors of difficulty and danger."

—John Gill

HUBRIS

A lot of climbing is about believing in oneself. Think about it: Men and women of little egos would have trouble convincing themselves to solve difficult problems in frightening places. The annals of climbing are rife with statements of sweeping confidence and opinionated references to various climbers' exaggerated sense of greatness—a common character profile of the personalities drawn to climbing. Most climbers at one time or another are no doubt guilty of this exaggerated sense of self-worth, and it would be difficult for any climber not to clash with (his own or) other climbers' egos along the way. Aside from my own youthful episodes of swagger, my most memorable experience with hubris occurred in 1979, in the Canadian Rockies.

My partner Chip Woodland and I had been kept awake much of the previous night by two arrogant guides loudly chattering in the tiny Cooper Hut. Chip and I were vying for one particular north face route on Mount Fay that the guides wanted to themselves, but because we left earlier in the morning, we got to the route first. They climbed another route up the face.

Later that afternoon, during our descent down the Kallen Couloir, the two guides lost their footing and fell the length of the couloir (which we had politely asked them to avoid descending while we were in it): their climbing rope flossed me off and I slid 500 feet. Miraculously, I was unhurt; the two guides—who had slid, rolled, and bounced 1,500 feet—had some crampon lacerations, bruises, and sprung ligaments. After carefully inspecting them for more serious bodily injury, neither of them offered an apology, so I gave them a long lecture about safety and their rude behavior the night before. They walked down with pronounced limps.

The leader of the two guides, James (who wore a golfing cap instead of a helmet), so far condescended as to present me with new crampons and ice ax pick (from the guiding school equipment locker)—both broken in the fall. We thought that was the last we would see of James, a legend in his own mind.

Six years later, while wandering across Alberta's Wapta Icefields in a whiteout of cloud, looking for a hard-to-find hut, I hailed a group of climbers. None of them answered. When I drew within talking distance, it was apparent that one of the climbers was a guide, lecturing his deferential group of clients. I asked if they knew the way to the hut, and the guide (who looked familiar) instead of answering, turned to his clients and rolled his eyes, as if I was the textbook example of how a turkey gets lost in a whiteout. The clients were all smiling at me as if they had identified the silent farter at their tea party. When the guide turned back to me, wearing that unmistakable golfing cap cocked at a jaunty angle, I recognized him immediately.

"James," I said, "You might remember me from Mount Fay?"

As recognition flashed across the neurons of his memory bank, he flinched, blanched, then opened his mouth in speechless wonder. As he tried to regain his composure, I walked away. The look of recognition on his face, in some small way, made up for the hubris that had nearly ruined my best summer of climbing.

"We have reached the summit of Mount McKinley by a new route in the north, and have mapped 3,000 miles of new country."

—**Frederick Cook's** fraudulent claim, from a letter to H. L. Bridgman.

≍

"Mount McKinley has attracted ego maniacs of all stripes."

—**David Roberts**

≍

"Outside the world of magazines and beyond the egos, a couple of million mountaineers are having a ball."

—**John Barry**

≍

"I piss on you all from a considerable height."

—**Céline**

≍

"We're on top of this fucker."

—**Kim Momb,** radioing from Everest's summit down to the East Face base camp.

"Only the pure climb gracefully."

—Anonymous

≍

"As for the top climbers, I'd say the U.S. scene is lackadaisical. We were at Smith Rock the other day where good climbers were working a route on the top rope that was climbed ten years ago."

—**Scott Franklin**

≍

"Have you had enough of my character? Do you feel willing once more or have you had enough of expeditions and of my not too easy disposition during the journeys?"

—**The Duke of Abruzzi's** letter to Vittorio Sella, inviting him to K2 in 1909.

≍

"If people don't believe me, that's their problem."

—**Tomo Cesen,** commenting on his fraudulent solo of the South Face of Lhotse in 1990.

"This is my last great alpine dream. Indeed it is the last great alpine idea."

—**Reinhold Messner,** speaking about his unsupported Nanga Parbat solo.

≍

"You suck . . . There, it's done. I've finally vented the words that have been stewing inside me for weeks. Now I'll be tarred, feathered, and deported back to England. But what the hell. I've got your attention, and we can discuss why American rock climbers have fallen so far behind their European counterparts in the last fifteen years, and what, if anything, you can do about it."

—**Dave Pegg's** lead from an article in *Climbing* magazine.

≍

"Don't forget, it's really just a big pile of rocks."

—Three-time summiteer **David Breashears's** aphorism at Everest base camp to those who had not yet climbed the mountain.

"Hi.

Im a 22 yr old MALE Looking FOR 1 or 2 FEMALES
BETWEEN 17-27 FOR A MEANINGFUL RELATION-
SHIP. MUST BE —GOOD LOOKING—5.4"- 5.9"
—BLOND, RED HEAD/FUCK I DON'T CARE
—LIKES BEING PUT IN THE
submissive POSITION. REPLY ON BOARD!"

> —From the bulletin board at Joshua Tree.

≍

"Great. Now I have to sit here and listen to fifty guys tell me
how they're going to do the route."

> —**Steve Hong,** separated from the climbing wall
> during a competition.

≍

"That's the risk you take when you go climbing."

> —To Sibylle Hechtel, from an anonymous woman
> who knocked off rocks in Eldorado Canyon and
> nearly killed several climbers.

≍

"Are you sure? It's not that hard."

> —**Peter Habeler,** above an overhang on Mount
> Moran, talking down to George Lowe, who asked
> for a rope.

"Do you think my climb will be counted as the first Italian success?"

> —**Claudio Corti,** after being rescue-winched up the North Face of the Eiger and losing his partner (see "Epics").

⋈

"Those guys had the worst attitudes. I don't think they even climb that hard."

> —Hueco Tanks climber, who overheard a group of disgruntled climbers talking about rules to the park rangers.

⋈

"Pig."

> —**John Roskelley,** addressing the Northeast Face of Tawoche in the Himalayas.

⋈

"Those are the bones of the last sixteen-year-old girl that came here and on-sighted [5].12d."

> —**Chris Righter,** to young Katie Brown, asking about the contents of a nearby bag after she had just completed a climb which he could not.

"To the untrained eye, selfish or ego climbing and selfless climbing may appear identical. Both kinds of climber place one foot in front of the other. Both breathe in and out at the same rate. Both stop when tired. Both go forward when rested. But what a difference! The ego climber is like an instrument that's out of adjustment. He puts his foot down an instant too soon or late. He's likely to miss a beautiful passage of sunlight through the trees. He goes on when the sloppiness of his step says he's tired. He rests at odd times. He looks up the trail trying to see what's ahead even when he knows what's ahead because he just looked a second before. He goes too fast or too slow for the conditions and when he talks his talk is forever about something else. He's here but he's not here."

—**Robert Pirsig,** author of *Zen and the Art of Motorcycle Maintenance.*

≍

"The fact that I'm three months pregnant doesn't change anything."

—**Catherine Destivelle,** preparing to solo the Old Man of Hoy seastack.

≍

"In some ways, they consider me a local."

—**Alan Burgess,** referring to how the Sherpas respect him.

"What have you guys got around here worth climbing?"

—Newcomer **Royal Robbins,** addressing Yosemite
locals in the early 1950s.

≍

"Now I'm off to Mendoza to settle my book, and make those
men pay for doubting the Fitzgerald expedition."

—**Mattias Zurbriggen,** atop the 22,310-foot
Tupungato in Chile, 1897.

≍

"Such arrogance, I believe, is dangerous for any climber, but it
is especially dangerous for one who purports to be a
Himalayan guide."

—**Jon Krakauer,** answering charges from Himalayan
guide Anatoli Boukreev during their Internet
squabble about the 1996 Everest disaster.

≍

"Awww, man! You can't make it up *that*! If you can't tick that
route, dude, you should just walk away and sell your gear. No
wait, forget selling it: if you can't send that route, just leave
your gear where it is and *give* it away to the next guy that comes
along."

—**Marc Dube** raving about Walk on the Wild Side,
5.11c, Grotto Canyon.

"The credit will read 'photograph of Ed Webster by Ed Webster,' right?"

>—**Bryan Becker,** photographing Ed with the latter's camera.

≍

"Shut up you chickenshit."

>—**Frank Sacherer,** to his belayer, Eric Beck, who had requested that more protection be put in on the lead.

≍

"We wouldn't have so many badly bolted routes up at the pass if people weren't so motivated by their egos."

>—**David Hale,** at an Aspen meeting about climbing ethics.

"If it weren't for egos, some of the greatest accomplishments in climbing would never have happened."

>—**Michael Kennedy,** responding to Hale's comment.

≍

"He is not as handsome as me."

>—**Heinrich Harrer,** lecturing at the Banff Film Festival about Brad Pitt's limitations in playing the Austrian mountain climber.

HUMILITY

"And up on the mountain we began our ant-like labours. What is a man on an ice-world up in the sky? At that altitude he is no more than a will straining in a spent machine."

—Gaston Rébuffat

HUMILITY

If hubris is the yin of climbing, humility is the yang. Although attempting 100-degree angled stone, or a 3,000-foot granite wall, or an 8,000-meter peak demands some level of swaggering panache and self-confidence, such an experience also forces an overwhelming sense of humility onto a climber. After all, one becomes terribly small against the infinite face of nature.

No climbers described humility better than those who suffered from frostbite and snowblindness while climbing Annapurna in 1950. Maurice Herzog's celebrated book *Annapurna* (ten million copies were sold and translated into dozens of languages) is a timeless account of mountaineering humility. This small French team single-handedly reconnoitered then climbed the first 8,000-meter peak—several years before Everest was climbed.

Herzog and Louis Lachenal summited, but at great cost because their ensuing bivouac caused severe frostbite. Herzog dictated the book from his hospital bed, where he spent months recovering from the amputation of his toes. He may have understated how much his companion (similarly frostbitten) figured into his salvation, but no one will ever accuse the men of not having suffered dearly. Lachenal's recently published diaries, *Carnets du Vertige,* while refuting Herzog's nationalism and presenting an account that is often at odds with the classic *Annapurna,* is nonetheless a similar account of humility.

Lachenal, the experienced Chamonix guide, wrote about accompanying the amateur Herzog to the summit: "I didn't owe my feet to the Youth of France. . . . I thought that if he continued alone, he would never return. It was for him and him alone that I did not turn back." Lachenal (a taciturn man uninterested in glory or honors) received none of the media adulation that Herzog did, and, according to another Annapurna teammate, Lionel Terray, Lachenal lost his "genius" as a climber along with the amputation of his toes. He became famous for his reckless driving and auto accidents, then was killed in a skiing accident five years after their famous climb. Terray died in a climbing accident in 1965. Another Annapurna teammate, Gaston Rébuffat (see opening quote) before dying of cancer in 1985, went on to write a number of beautiful books about climbing technique, camaraderie, and humility.

Herzog, at the time of this writing, is the only surviving member of the 1950 climb. He has seen to the care of Terray's and Lachenal's families, and is stung by Lachenal's and Rébuffat's differences of opinions. But no one can deny the power of his romantic book, the last line of which presents the most unforgettable humility, "There are other Annapurnas in the lives of men."

▲ ▲ ▲

"I have *conquaired zee* mountain St. Elias, but *zee* mosquitoes have *conquaired* me."

— **The Duke of Abruzzi,** in reply to an American climber's congratulations in 1897.

≍

"Humility is the key to being a good alpinist."

— **Barry Blanchard**

≍

"My Alaskan climbs were really just polar explorations with three dimensions."

— **Bradford Washburn**

≍

"I don't worry about ratings too much. I figure there's only three basic categories for climbing: 5.easy, 5.fun, and 5.hard. The rest is just numbers."

— **Brian Cox**

≍

"My ambition was to become the best climber and I never did."

— **Royal Robbins**

"You cannot stay on the summit forever,
You have to come down again....
So why bother in the first place?
Just this: what is above knows what is below;
But what is below does not know what is above.
One climbs, one sees. One descends, one sees no longer,
But one has seen. There is an art of conducting oneself
in the lower regions by the memory of what one saw
higher up."

—**René Dumal**

≍

"Just Do It is basically [5.]13c to a really big rest, then maybe
14a after that."

—Sixteen-year-old **Chris Sharma's** comment on being
the first American to repeat the difficult route
(considered one of only two 5.14c's in the U.S.) at
Smith Rocks.

≍

"I don't want to overstate my rock climbing ability. I choose
my routes pretty carefully. I always go with people who can
catch me."

—**Tom Brokaw,** television journalist.

"Half the fun and half the challenge of photographing big walls is the torture."

—**Greg Epperson**

≍

"I'm just a Walter Mitty."

—**Sandy Pittman,** before her third attempt on Everest.

≍

"I am too slow to be good climber, so I film instead."

—**Wanda Rutkiewicz,** who had climbed numerous 8,000-meter peaks, often without oxygen.

≍

"Everything was cold, even our souls. We were drawing heavily on all of our Himalayan experience just to survive and it was a respectful pair that finally stood on the summit ridge."

—**Dougal Haston,** on the first alpine style ascent of Denali's South Face in 1976.

≍

"Climbing mountains must never degenerate into an ascetic discipline!"

—**J. H. B. Bell**

"And what joy, think ye, did they feel after the exceeding long and troublous ascent?—After scrambling, slipping, pulling, pushing, lifting, gasping, looking, hoping, despairing, climbing, holding on, falling off, trying, puffing, loosing, gathering, talking, stepping, grumbling, anathematizing, scraping, hacking, bumping, jogging, overturning, hunting, standing,—for know ye that by these methods alone are the most divine mysteries of the Quest revealed?"

> —**Norman Collie,** on Scotland's Tower Ridge in
> winter.

≍

"The best climber in the world is the one who's having the most fun."

> —**Alex Lowe,** the best climber in the world.

≍

"I have not conquered Everest, it has merely tolerated me."

> —**Peter Habeler,** after climbing that mountain
> without bottled oxygen.

≍

"A lot of us became famous without even knowing it."

> —**Jim Bridwell**

"The tops of mountains are among the unfinished parts of the globe, whither it is a slight insult to the gods to climb and pry into their secrets, and try their effect on our humanity. Only daring and insolent men, perchance, go there. Simple races, as savages, do not climb mountains—their tops are sacred and mysterious tracts never visited by them."

—**Henry David Thoreau,** on his climb of Katahdin.

≍

"I don't really think about how good I am, 'cause often you have to compare yourself to other people. And I don't want to do that."

—Fifteen-year-old **Katie Brown,** on her wishes not to become the star of the well-televised Extreme Games (which she handily won).

≍

"Now I'm just acutely aware of how far from perfect my mountaineering ability is, and how even a pretty small mistake can be disastrous in the Alaska Range."

—**Glenn Randall,** after climbing a new route on Mount Foraker, falling, and being rescued with pulmonary and cerebral edema, cracked ribs, a broken leg, and sprained ankles.

"If only he could get to know the mountains better and let them become a part of him, he would lose much of his aggression. The struggle of man against man produces jealousy, deceit, frustration, bitterness, hate. The struggle of man against the mountains is different. . . . Man then bows before something that is bigger than he. When he does that, he finds serenity and humility and dignity too."

  —William O'Douglas

≌

"Indeed we were waxen weary; but who heedeth weariness Who hath been all day on the mountain?"

  —Geoffrey Winthrop Young

≌

"I don't know who was the conqueror or who was conquered. I do recall that El Cap seemed to be in much better condition than I was."

  —Warren Harding, after his first ascent of the Nose in 1958.

≌

"Climbing may be hard . . .
 but it's easier than growing up."

  —Tee-shirt conceived by Ed Sklar.

"For those long days we were within the scheme of things, that short time of movement among the rock and ice which allows us to live through the rest of the year."

—**Dave Seidman,** on the first ascent of Denali's South Face.

≍

"In my dreams I glissade delightfully, but in practice I find that somehow the snow will not behave properly and that my alpenstock will get between my legs."

—**Edward Whymper**

≍

"They greeted us by taking our outstretched hands in both of theirs and bowing. How vulgar is our European handshake compared with this Tibetan greeting in which trust, respect, and friendship are combined. It is not our race that has kept the secret of grace and distinction."

—**René Dittert**

≍

"Something besides courage and determination is needed to climb a mountain like this. Forgive me if I call it intelligence."

—**Robert Dunn,** on his 1903 attempt to climb Denali.

"The true result of endeavour, whether on a mountain or in any context, may be found in its lasting effects rather than in the few moments during which a summit is trampled by mountain boots. The real measure is the success or fall of the climber to triumph, not over a lifeless mountain, but over himself: the true value of the enterprises lies in the example to others of human motivation and human contact."

—**Sir John Hunt**

⋈

"I seemed to discover the deep significance of existence of which till then I had been unaware. I saw that it was better to be true than to be strong. The marks of my ordeal are apparent on my body. I was saved and had won my freedom. This freedom, which I shall never lose, has given me the assurance and serenity of a man who has fulfilled himself. It has given me the rare joy of loving that which I used to despise. A new and splendid life has opened out before me."

—**Maurice Herzog,** from the *Hôpital Américan de Paris in 1951.*

THE GREAT DIVIDE

"Climb if you will, but remember that courage and strength are nothing without prudence, and that a momentary negligence may destroy the happiness of a lifetime."

—**Edward Whymper,** after his rope broke on the Matterhorn.

THE GREAT DIVIDE

Ever since four of Edward Whymper's companions fell to their deaths in 1865, no climber remains unaffected by those who are killed while climbing. John Donne's, "Never send to know for whom the bell tolls; it tolls for thee" is relevant because the climbing community is small, and because most every well-traveled climber will eventually lose a friend.

As for fatality statistics, on Everest, the highest mountain in the world, three percent of the total number of climbers are actually killed; on Denali, highest in North America, less than a half percent of the climbers die. Rock climbing, however, is a safer game than alpinism. In the mountains, it is generally thought that objective dangers or acts of God (avalanches, storms, or falling rock) are the rarest method of departure, and that most climbers die because of subjective mistakes (extending their abilities, altitude sickness, falling, or inexperience).

Other potentially fatal outdoor activities—such as sailing, surfing, or skiing (which kills one in a million people)—are largely lacking in the macabre humor that surrounds climbing. Sweeping understatements and nonchalant shrugs about *getting chopped* are part of the lexicon of most climbers. Death in fact is such an accepted part of more difficult climbs, that alpinists commonly make out their wills before certain climbs, then joke about who gets their gear when they're gone. A popular tee-shirt in the 1980s read: "He who dies with the most toys wins." However, after the death of a partner, or a close call, climbers will occasionally speak seriously about the likelihood of dying at their chosen game.

▲ ▲ ▲

"Take me home, I don't want to die."

> —**John Mallon Waterman,** to a bush pilot after his
> failed solo attempt of Denali in winter 1979.

≍

"I want to see if I'm afraid to die."

> —**Layton Kor,** before attempting Yosemite's Steck-
> Salathé in winter 1963.

≍

"Death is chasing me in this country. I have to leave before it
catches me."

> —**Gary Hemming,** before he committed suicide in the
> Tetons.

≍

"It was worth dying on the mountain to leave a reputation like
that."

> —London *Times* epitaph for Sandy Irvine, who
> disappeared with Mallory on Everest.

≍

"In the Alps, man proposes, weather disposes."

> —**George D. Abraham**

"It was almost the six-foot dirt nap."

> —**Scott Backes,** after a multi-ton vertical ice pillar
> broke beneath his feet and crashed to the river
> below.

≍

"I think that is really a good mix of guides because if there is
a problem on summit day there would not be any issue or
question."

> —**Scott Fischer,** referring to his choice of Neil
> Beidleman and Anatoli Boukreev for their 1996
> climb.

≍

"If I fall off a mountain, to me it does not mean a thing. I come
off, maybe five more seconds, and then I am dead. It's my wife,
it's my two boys that are left behind."

> —**Peter Habeler**

≍

"I am lost."

> —**Naomi Uemura's** last words over the radio, while
> descending from the summit of Denali (McKinley) in
> February 1984, after completing the first winter solo.

In 1977, **Nanda Devi Unsoeld,** at 24,000 feet on the mountain she was named after, suddenly sat up in her tent after an illness and said: "I am going to die." (She then immediately succumbed in her father's arms.)

"Andy, Peter and I knelt in a circle in the snow and grasped hands while each chanted a broken farewell to the comrade who had so recently filled such a vivid place in our lives. My final prayer was one of thanksgiving for a world filled with the sublimity of the high places, for the sheer beauty of the mountains and for the surpassing miracle that we should be so formed as to respond with ecstasy to such beauty, and for the constant element of danger without which the mountain experience would not exercise such a grip on our sensibilities. We then laid the body to rest in its icy tomb, at rest on the breast of the Bliss-Giving Goddess Nanda."

—**Willi Unsoeld,** burying his daughter.

≍

"In my end is my beginning."

—**Mary,** Queen of Scots, 1542–1587.

≍

"The dead being the majority, it is natural that we should have more friends among them than among the living."

—**Samuel Butler,** English novelist.

"The true alpinist is the man who attempts new ascents."

—**Albert F. Mummery,** who disappeared on the
unclimbed Nanga Parbat in 1895.

≍

"People got killed climbing with fixed ropes and without fixed
ropes; people got killed at the top of the mountain and the
bottom; old people got killed and young people got killed. If
anything was common to most of the deaths it was that a lot
of people were very ambitious and had a lot to gain by climbing K2 and a lot to lose as well. Casarotto, the Austrians, Al
Rouse, the Barrards were all—the word that comes to mind is
overambitious. I think if you're going to try alpine-style
ascents of 8,000-meter peaks you've got to leave yourself room
to fail."

—**Jim Curran,** writing about the disastrous summer of
1986 on K2.

≍

"Remember not to have a fatal accident, because the community will think climbing is a dangerous thing, your friends will
be bummed . . . and you'll be dead."

—**Kitty Calhoun,** closing remarks at an American
Alpine Club lecture.

"Knowing death is his end,
Death he weighs in his hand.
Where the ice ridges bend,
Where the feat's pride is his friend,
Straight let him stand."

> —**Wilfrid Noyce,** composing during the 1953 Everest
> expedition about how to face death; he died
> climbing nine years later in the Pamirs.

⊁

"As most of these know nothing of the technique of getting killed, the following rules may be of service, and are easily memorized: A fascinating way is to go and pick edelweiss. To pluck it one must approach from above. Descend slowly, therefore, clinging to some small shrub. If a passing guide chances to call warning, reply that you know what you are about, and that tourists, as well as guides, have a right to pick alpine flowers. Lean slightly over the precipice, and as one hand grasps the alluring bloom, with the other hand pull hard on the shrub, which will come loose, roots and all! There will be a grating sound of loose, moving rock, the overhanging ledge will cave in, and one may soar, edelweiss in hand, into the void below. There will be three lines in the newspapers about it, and a caravan of expert guides will find the body."

> —**Frederick Burlingham**

"Alone, their last desperate chance now gone, the men relinquished the fragile thread of life."

> —**Howard Snyder,** lamenting the deaths of his seven companions on Denali in 1967.

≍

"It was just a snow avalanche. Hey, Boyd! Hey, Dave! Hey, Vin! I'm alive and OK; here to dig you out. Just let me know where you are."

> —**Lou Reichardt,** in his diary about losing seven companions on Dhaulagiri.

≍

"I remember thinking that after that experience nothing would ever upset me again, I would be a different person, that I had been miraculously saved for some purpose I didn't understand. But it didn't take very long before I was back in the real world, a real person, and nothing much had changed."

> —**Dr. Charles Houston,** after losing his partner, Art Gilkey on K2 in 1953.

≍

"The Last Kiss"

> —**John Mallon Waterman's** final words scrawled on a cardboard box before he disappeared on Denali in 1982.

"Andy, of course, has the best possible excuse for not being here."

—**Jim Curran**, accepting the Grand Prize at the Banff Book Festival, on behalf of author Andy Fanshawe, who was killed climbing.

≍

"There must be such an amazing awakening in death. I can't imagine that the supreme God is not realized, or at least in a way there is a true awakening that we are all a part of."

—Written by **Mugs Stump** shortly before he died climbing.

≍

"All the tents were flat, two bodies were lying nearby, all that showed of another body was this frozen 'and sticking out of the snow. The survivors said a fourth body was still buried somewhere, they didn't know where, and that a Tamang porter 'ad gone crazy after the avalanche, thrown off all 'is clothes, and run off into the night. All I could think was, *Oh man, is this shit really 'appening?*"

—**Al Burgess,** on surviving a large snowfall in the Khumbu Himalaya.

"Goretta, I have fallen. I am dying. Please send help. Quickly!"

—Soloist **Renato Casarotto,** talking to his wife over the radio after falling into a crevasse beneath K2; he died shortly after being pulled out.

≍

"Goddamn it! His parka doesn't fit me!"

—While climbing past Irving Smith's body, **Steve Roper** breaks the tension to Yvon Chouinard.

≍

"Now we are two. And now we will all die. We are very sorry. We tried but we could not. . . . Please forgive us. We love you. Good-bye."

—A team of eight Russian women, led by **Elvira,** radioing from the summit of Peak Lenin in a storm.

≍

"Hey, look, don't worry too much about me."

—**Rob Hall's** last words, through a satellite radio-phone below Everest's summit to his pregnant wife, Jan Arnold, in New Zealand.

"When it's your time to go, it's your time to go and there's nothing you can do about it."

> —**Dan Reid,** quoted during a dangerous crossing of the "bowling alley" on Everest's East Face; he died several years later beneath Kilimanjaro.

≍

"The way I saw it, my life had been reduced to a handful of seconds, and now I had millions. I realized that everything I was doing had a freshness to it. A magic. The value I'd learned from Jonathan's death, and my own near-death, was that sense of moment. It's an incomparable scale to rate things by, to know what is and what is not a matter of consequence in your life."

> —**Rick Ridgeway,** on an avalanche and Jonathan Wright's death on Minya Konka.

≍

"I don't know how much satisfaction I'd get out of climbing K2 by a new route and then having my partner slip off during the descent and die. What good is that? You just can't do it over and over and over and expect to come out alive."

> —**Carlos Buhler**

"Hungry! Cold!"

  —The last words of **Stephano Longhi,** carried by the
winds across the North Face of the Eiger.

     ≍

"What's fame after all? 'Tis apt to be what someone writes on
your tombstone."

  —**Finley Peter Dunne,** American humorist.

     ≍

"Some say that the best climbers are the ones that are alive."

  —**Eric DeCamp**

     ≍

"When you die it negates the whole game: you haven't just
fucked yourself, you've hurt lots of other people—that's when
it becomes irresponsible and tragic."

  —**Greg Child**

     ≍

"The report of my death was an exaggeration."

  —**Mark Twain**

"I can do no more."

—**Toni Kurz's** last words on the North Face of the
Eiger while trying to untie a knot in order that his
rescuers could reach him.

≍

"Oh shit!"

—**Jim Madsen's** anguished cry as he rappelled off the
rope end and fell 2,500 feet down El Capitan.

≍

"Well, you might live longer, but at least I'll die with a full
rack."

—**Craig Smith,** arguing about rappel anchors with his
partner, who wanted to leave another stopper.

GEARING UP

"A perfection of means and confusion of aims seems to be our main problem."

—**Albert Einstein,** quoted in *The Chouinard Catalog, 1972.*

GEARING UP

Even in the early days of alpinism, when tweed-jacketed alpinists had seemingly primitive gear (by today's standards), it was not uncommon for them to carry wine bottles, heavy theodolites, silk tents, barometers, sextants, telescopes, or iron bedsteads. Modern climbers are no longer so burdened because satellite GPS's, titanium ice screws, aluminum carabiners, synthetic clothing, and freeze-dried food are all so lightweight. However, in relative terms, pioneers and modernists are remarkably alike in their technophilia.

Next to the obsession with actual climbing beta (route details), climbing banter has *always* been about equipment: what protection a particular pitch demands, the latest stove, the lightest tent, the most functional ice ax (or alpenstock), or the best handling rope (or hemp). Although it is a recent phenomenon in the U.S., hundreds of climbers now make their livelihood, or at least receive free gear, from equipment companies. Climbers looking for sponsors and new gear crowd the biannual Outdoor Retailer show in Salt Lake City (or various trade shows around the world), salivating over hundreds of manufacturers' booths that display the latest technological advances in equipment.

Throughout this traditional pastime of gear fondling, and balanced by the necessity of carrying the right stuff, there has always been a camp of climbers who advocate "pure" style, that is, a minimum of equipment and technologic aid. Various ethical controversies have raged on and off since the beginning of alpinism: climbing without oxygen, climbing free versus climbing with direct equipment aid, banning bolts (after pitons were successfully banned), dispensing with fixed ropes, or eschewing airplane and radio support. The uniting philosophy of equipment purists is that most technology reduces the mountain and separates climbers from the challenge of their routes. However, it's a tough balance, because carrying the proper equipment is also equal to a climber's safety.

In 1995, a partner and I attempted an unclimbed route on Mount St. Elias. We had minimal equipment sponsorship, and mostly wore clothing and equipment we had used on previous climbs. We carried no radio or GPS, skied in from the sea fifty miles (rather than using airplane support), and took no fixed ropes. Although our minimalist philosophy may have had a lot to do with forcing us off the mountain before summiting (we probably would have succeeded with airplane support), one climber recently called our small "alpine-style" team—with its lack of gear and support—foolhardy. In the end, we have the peace of mind of knowing that we made it halfway up the mountain because of our own pluck and abilities. And not because of equipment.

▲ ▲ ▲

"The rope should, indeed, be regarded by each member of the party, exclusively as an aid and protection to his companions. Those who feel its constant use essential to their own comfort, should regard this as indisputable evidence that they are engaging in expeditions too difficult for them; a practice which will never make good and self-reliant climbers."

—**Albert F. Mummery**

≍

"Think of everything you could possibly want on a climbing expedition, say, of thirty hours. Cut out from this all that you think might be fairly easily dispensed with. Take with you 50 per cent of the remainder."

—**Harold Raeburn**

≍

"Today's climber carries his courage in his rucksack, in the form of bolts and equipment."

—**Reinhold Messner**

≍

"The sort of man who would drive a piton into English rock, is the sort of man who would shoot a fox."

—1930s anonymous adage.

"Change is inevitable. It is what tradition in climbing is all about."

> —**Alan Watts,** talking about power drill bolting and hangdogging tactics in order to climb 5.14 in the 1980s.

≍

"John Wayne never wore Lycra."

> —**Ron Kauk,** in blue jeans, commenting on the proliferation of Lycra-clad sport climbers ("Eurodogs") at the Stonemasters' climbing competition at Mount Woodson in 1987. Kauk won.

≍

"Dancing on ice with V.B.'s [floppy boots], snow crampons, an ax that won't stick, no hammer and 60 lb. pack demands concentration."

> —**Brian Okonek's** journal entry during first ascent (and in winter) of Mount Foraker's Sultana Ridge, 1979.

≍

"I ♣ my car"

> —Homemade bumper sticker seen on abused Honda at the trailhead for Slesse Mountain.

"Ed Viesturs didn't bring oxygen to the top of Mount Everest. But he did bring VO2MAX®."

> —Magazine advertisement about a Mars® food bar and Ed Viesturs, "the only American to climb ten of the world's fourteen peaks over 26,000 feet without supplemental oxygen."

≍

"These days, instead of taking emergency bivouac gear, guys go out on hard climbs and take nothing but a radio. If things get sketchy they assume they can just get on the horn and call for a rescue."

> —**John Bouchard,** owner and chief innovator of Wild Things equipment.

≍

"Simplicity in life is important; that is where it is at for me."

> —**Guy Lacelle,** the smoothest ice technician in the world, on equipment minimalism.

≍

"There would seem to be little doubt that had we not left ropes in place during the ascent we would be there somewhere on the mountain hanging from the unprotected ridge like sides of mutton."

> —**Dave Nichols,** on a retreat from a Patagonian summit.

"If you don't take care of yourself, the best equipment in the world can't prevent frostbite."

—**Jonathan Waterman,** from *Surviving Denali.*

≍

"The trend is toward less and less equipment. People are giving up this, and giving up that, and trying to get back to their roots. It takes you back to what I see as the ultimate in free climbing: the unroped, nude, solo climber. The closer you can come to approximating this, without killing yourself, the more you'll get out of climbing."

—**Jim Erikson,** 1970s trailblazer.

≍

"When we started we made stuff for ourselves and a few friends. Things haven't changed much in the last 20 years— we just have more friends."

—Patagonia advertisement in *Climbing* magazine, 1995.

≍

"So what's it like being sponsored by Petzl?"

—**Rob De Conto,** to teenagers at Colorado climbing area Shelf Road wearing his tights, quickdraws, and pack—stolen two weeks earlier from the back of his truck.

"Climbers will eventually need to buy safety equipment including a harness and shock bag."

—*Be Healthy* magazine, March 1994.

≍

"Facing death by avalanche, why did I choose to be buried in these clothes?"

—**Jeff Lowe,** in a magazine advertisement for Polartec, with the small explanatory print: "when the snow hit, his mind stayed calm because he knew his body would stay warm."

≍

"Supposing it was the regular thing for all mountaineers to use pitons on their climbs, would it not be a sign of the degeneracy of man?"

—**Frank S. Smythe,** 1940s.

≍

"This is not the sort of gadget to inspire nursery rhymes. I look at the DMM Predator ice ax and I think of murder."

—**Stephen King,** horror writer.

≍

"You will die before your Verve pants do."

—Magazine advertisement for that company.

"We might as well divide up his gear."

   —A partner of Don Goodrich, who was killed from a
   fall on Mount Conness in 1959.

≍

"Equipment has little to do with the quality of the adventure.
For that we ask: is there a bold line, uncertainty, objective danger, isolation, and the need for self-reliance?"

   —**Todd Thompson**

≍

"At altitude, supplemental oxygen makes it possible for an
individual who is not prepared physically or mentally to step
over the border of his own limits and to wander unaware in
the Death Zone."

   —**Anatoli Boukreev**

≍

"Gravity sucks"

   —No Fear advertisement in a magazine.

FEMALE INSPIRATION

"Although one is not inclined to be timid or nervous, it is nevertheless a trifle depressing to receive letters full of expostulation and entreaty: 'If you are determined to commit suicide, why not come home and do so in a quiet lady-like manner?'"

—**Anne Smith Peck,** July 1896.

FEMALE INSPIRATION

It is often observed today that those women (or men) at the top of their form in climbing are not trying to be spokespersons for their sex, let alone any particular movement, so much as they are trying to simply attain their own personal best and advance the state of the art for all people. But this was not always true in climbing.

Before the turn of the century, the phrase "an easy day for a lady" implied that a climb was no longer a challenge for serious climbers. The Englishwoman Lily Bristow however, came to deflate this phrase not only by outclimbing men, but by not hiring guides. She often climbed with Alfred Mummery and his wife, who wrote in 1895: "The slopes of the Breithorn and the snows of the Weisshorn are usually supposed to mark the limit of ascents suitable to the weaker sex—indeed, strong prejudices are apt to be aroused the moment a woman attempts any more formidable sort of mountaineering. It appears to me, however, that her powers are, in actual fact, better suited to the really difficult climbs than to the monotonous snow grinds usually considered more fitting. Really difficult ascents are of necessity made at a much slower pace, halts are fairly frequent, and, with few exceptions, the alternations of heat and cold are less extreme. Snow grinds, on the contrary, usually involve continuous and severe exertion—halts on a wide snowfield are practically impossible—and the danger of frostbite in the early morning is succeeded by the certainty of sunburning at midday."

Miriam O'Brian was the first American woman to take up the torch of manless climbing in the Alps in the early twentieth century, if only because she wanted to lead, rather than following on the heels of a chivalrous male. After getting married, she merely revised her manless concept to "guideless" climbing and went on to climb many of the hardest rock routes of the day in the Alps. Ultimately, Miriam and her husband (Robert Underhill) were the people who introduced the United States to formerly unknown rope and belay techniques.

In the footsteps of the Underhills at the millennium, Lynn Hill has shown the world about the frontiers of climbing by freeing the Nose of El Capitan—a feat that no man or woman has yet repeated. Another breaker of barriers is the Frenchwoman Catherine Destivelle (a former competitor of Hill's in sport climbing competitions), who has amassed an amazing array of solo, winter, and first free ascents in the Alps, the Himalayas, and Antarctica. And on the heels of Bristow, O'Brian, Hill, and Destivelle, other women (like the extraordinary and young rock climber Katie Brown) will continue to redefine the frontiers of climbing.

▲ ▲ ▲

"Non Mademoiselle, pas possible!"

—Nineteenth-century hotel staff to Lily Bristow, when
told she had just climbed the Rothhorn *sans* guides.

≍

"I was going again because I had need of courage and inspiration and because on the high mountains I find them as
nowhere else."

—**Dora Keen,** on first ascent of Blackburn, 1913.

≍

"I think I was a little drunk on the air up there, but it was beautiful being on top. Vague and indistinct, fabled peaks rose out
of the ice and rock below."

—**Shari Kearney,** atop Mount Hunter after her first
ascent of the Southwest Ridge.

≍

."Up and up in my estimation went every iceman in the world,
for ice, I discovered, is one of the hardest and toughest mate-
rials in existence."

—**Betsy Cowles,** learning how to ice climb in
Switzerland, 1936.

"The woman in the 100-meter run is one second less than the man. That doesn't mean that she's worse."

—**Wanda Rutkiewicz,** Polish alpinist.

≍

"As for Mont Blanc: 'Why, then, do we not go up?' you say. As to us ladies, it is a thing that has been done only by two women since the world stood, and those very different in their physique from any we are likely to raise in America, unless we mend our manners very much. Then, as to the gentlemen, it is a serious consideration, in the first place, that the affair costs about one hundred and fifty dollars apiece, takes two days a time, uses up a week's strength, all to get an experience of some very disagreeable sensations, which could not afflict a man in any case."

—**Harriet Beecher Stowe,** 1853.

≍

"They heard I had climbed a few mountains in Alaska. They said it would be a better movie if they had a girl in it."

—**Barbara Washburn,** talking about RKO Radio
Pictures including her in a promotional
documentary film about climbing Denali in 1947,
as a gimmick to promote the Hollywood feature
film, *The White Tower.*

"The masculine mind, however, is, with rare exceptions, imbued with the idea that a woman is not a fit comrade for steep ice or precipitous rock, and, in consequence, holds it as an article of faith that her climbing should be done by Mark Twain's method, and that she should be satisfied with watching through a telescope some weedy and invertebrate masher being hauled up a steep peak by a couple of burly guides, or by listening to this same masher when, on his return, he lisps out with a Sickening drawl the many perils he has encountered."

—**Mrs. A. F. Mummery,** 1895 (the year her husband disappeared on Nanga Parbat).

≍

"I can't remember a single time that I was prevented from doing what I wanted because I was a female, either on the rock or in the mountains."

—**Annie Whitehouse**

≍

"I did the twenty-three-hour Nose route to the top of El Capitan in eighteen hours and twenty-three minutes, I can get over this."

—Avery Bishop (Kelly Preston) in response to *Jerry Maguire* (Tom Cruise) calling off their engagement.

"In common with many women, I felt that these Dolomites were made to suit me with their small but excellent toe- and finger-holds, and pitches where a delicate sense of balance was the key, rather than brute force. While it helps, of course, to have tough muscles, the prizefighter would not necessarily make a fine Dolomite climber. But the ballet dancer might."

—**Miriam Underhill,** first American woman to
espouse both manless and guideless climbing.

≍

"I'm three for three on 8000ers. Pretty damn good odds."

—**Charlotte Fox,** guided client on Cho Oyu,
Gasherbrum, and Everest.

≍

"On the first morning, I took them up Middlefell Buttress: five of us, all on one rope. It was slow, cold and boring. They climbed faster than I did, surrounded with an almost visible aura of masculine resentment. So I took them to Gwynne's Chimney on Pavey Ark, and as they struggled and sweated in that smooth cleft, sparks flying from their nails, and me waiting at the top with a taut rope and a turn round my wrist, I knew that I had won. The atmosphere—when we were all together again—was clean and relaxed."

—**Gwen Moffat,** climbing guide.

"She found being a woman and a climber to be easily congru-
ent."

> —**Annie Whitehouse,** talking about the alpinist
> Margaret Young.

≍

"A lady has clomb to the Matterhorn's summit,
Which almost like a monument points to the sky;
Steep not very much less than the string of a plummet
Suspended, which nothing can scale but a fly.

This lady has likewise ascended the Weisshorn,
And, what's a great deal more, descended it too,
Feet foremost; which, seeing it might be named Icehorn,
So slippery 'tis, no small thing to do.

No glacier can baffle, no precipice balk her,
No peak rise above her, however sublime.
Give three times three cheers for intrepid Miss Walker.
I say, my boys, doesn't she know how to climb!"

> —**Frederick Gardiner**

≍

"It is very important for women to climb with other women."

> —**Zoe Bundros,** on self-actualization as a climber.

"I came up to help you with your pack, but it looks like you don't need any help."

 —**John Roskelley**, to Deborah Waterman at 17,800 feet on Denali.

≍

"A Woman's Place Is on Top."

 —Popular late-1970s tee-shirt derived from an American woman's ascent of Annapurna.

≍

"A Woman's Place Is on the Face."

 —Follow-up to popular Annapurna tee-shirt in the 1980s.

≍

"Now, when she's not spending 11 hours a day teaching, Lisa is hard to pin down. You might find her at the gym, on a Colorado ski slope or in Europe, scaling a crag with her husband, Eric, a world-class climber."

 —*Playboy* magazine pictorial on Lisa Ann Hörst in her birthday suit.

≍

"The essence of climbing is not limited to those out there making a name for themselves."

 —**Lois LaRock**

"Technique and ability alone do not get you to the top—it is the willpower that is the most important. This willpower you cannot buy with money or be given by others—it rises from your heart."

> —**Junko Tabei,** after becoming the first woman to climb Everest in 1975.

≍

"I've never noticed that being a woman is a handicap or a plus. I am a woman and there are men and we climb together. Sometimes I'm stronger, sometimes they're stronger—we motivate each other."

> —**Robyn Erbesfield,** four-time World Cup winner.

≍

"No, she's the *leader* of our climb."

> —**Colin Grissom,** en route to Dhaulagiri, replying to a German climber who asked if the petite Kitty Calhoun was their base camp manager.

≍

"Never noticed a female monkey not climbing as well as a male, have you?"

> —**Don Whillans,** upon being asked if it was possible for a woman to be a better rock climber than a man.

RISK AND LUCK

"To have a great adventure, and survive, requires good judgment. Good judgment comes from experience. Experience, of course, is the result of poor judgment."

    —**Geoff Tabin**

RISK AND LUCK

Climbers are often loath to admit that they take chances. They prefer to credit their success to their own powers, rather than the serendipitous forces of the universe. As an Inuit upon the Beaufort Sea once corrected me (after I mistakenly wished him "good luck" on his coming seal hunt): "No, it is not luck that I have, but it is *skill.*"

Every climber, when pressed, can recount that experience of luck amid risk taking that saved their bacon. Maybe an avalanche that passes by minutes after you cross its slide path. Or topping out on a difficult route just before a blistering storm. Or rockfalls that inexplicably miss you by mere inches. Or a rope snagging on a bush during a long fall and preventing you from hitting the deck. Lightning striking all around you. These exact experiences of luck have all happened to me or my friends.

This so-called magic ingredient of luck, allows climbers to risk greatly again and again, and get away with it most of the time. Climbing alpine rock, remote waterfall ice, or big mountains is not blind risk taking so much as it is about a climber summoning forth intuition and experience to create their own luck. There are exceptions (like those listed above) of course, so-called acts of God which no climber can stop. But generally speaking, in climbing lexicon, *risk* usually refers more to the initial commitment than to the actual climb's dangers. For example, Paul Piana and Todd Skinner set out to free climb the Salathé Wall on El Capitan in late 1988. Amid the collective climber consciousness, Piana's and Skinner's risk was really about daring to set forth on a project (freeing the Salathé) that had only been previously aid climbed. In other words, their risk was thought to be mostly the risk of failure: they didn't know if they could climb a hard 5.13, thousands of feet above the deck. It was not so much about those acts of God or those perceived risks of rappelling off the end of the rope, or being beaned by a stray rock, or getting fried in an electric storm (even though a boulder rolled over them at the top of the climb).

So taking a risk is about conceptualizing and actualizing a "project" (read *climb*) to begin with. And luck is that which you help to create.

▲　▲　▲

"We knew that a failure on the first women's attempt on El Cap would be a fiasco we could never live down."

> —**Sibylle Hechtel,** after climbing The Triple Direct with Bev Johnson.

≍

"I worked myself into such a fevered pitch that I committed myself to the top portion and very fortunately made it."

> —**John Gill,** on the first ascent (solo) of the Thimble.

≍

"There is not enough luck in the world that I got somebody's share."

> —**Anatoli Boukreev,** after nearly dying while rescuing two climbers on Manaslu.

≍

"If ropes cost so much, why not use them?"

> —**Steve Wunsch,** on putting up scores of 5.11 routes in the early 1970s, and risking (not only falling a great deal) but the collective ethical wrath of climbers.

"There are old climbers and there are bold climbers, but there are no old, bold climbers."

—Anonymous

≍

"If you are not prepared to give a little credit to luck and chance, it would be better not to come to the Himalaya at all."

—**G. Chevalley**

≍

"To climb up rocks is like all the rest of your life, only simpler and safer."

—**Charles E. Montague**

≍

"But I do not believe in miracles."

—**Reinhold Messner,** after surviving Nanga Parbat and being told that it was a miracle.

≍

"We are lucky whether we believe in luck or not."

—**David Stevenson's** concluding sentence from his short story about an epic in the Cordillera Blanca.

"I do take various lucky charms with me on the wall, like this old ratty hex nut that I found on the Painted Wall in the Black Canyon in Gunnison, Colorado."

—**Mark Synnott,** hot young wall climber.

≍

"There are only three sports—mountain climbing, bullfighting, and motor racing—all the rest being games."

—**Ernest Hemingway**

≍

". . . like the jester sampling the king's food for poison."

—**Peter Boardman,** describing jumaring on a rope someone else has fixed.

≍

"He may, with the good luck which sometimes attends children, drunkards, and persons of weak intellect, escape the dangers without even knowing that they were there. But if he affronts too often forces whose powers he had not attempted to understand, he will in the long run succumb."

—**Lord Schuster**

"The truth is that we were all very, very lucky."

—**Marc Twight**, climbing floating icebergs in
Antarctica for a cigarette commercial.

≍

"If anything goes wrong it will be a fight to the end. If your
training is good enough, survival is there; if not, nature claims
its forfeit."

—**Dougal Haston**

≍

"The bizarre trend in mountaineers is not the risk they take,
but the large degree to which they value life. They are not crazy
because they don't dare, they're crazy because they do. These
people tend to enjoy life to the fullest, laugh the hardest, travel
the most, and work the least."

—**Lisa Morgan**

≍

"Our poignant adventure, our self-sought perils on a line of
unreason to the summit of a superfluous rock, have no rational or moral justification."

—**Geoffrey Winthrop Young**

"The secret of knowing the most fertile experiences and the greatest joys in life is to live dangerously."

—Friedrich Nietzsche

≍

While retreating down the North Face of the Eiger in a gray holocaust, **Don Whillans** tells two Japanese climbers who are foolishly still climbing: "You-may-be-going-up-Mate, but-a-lot-'igher-than-you-think!"

≍

"In the '60s, sex was safe and climbing was dangerous. Now it's the other way around."

—Chuck Pratt

≍

"Nothing in this game is without risk. We won't be able to make it one hundred percent safe."

—Kevin Sweigert, Hollywood climbing rigger.

≍

"Fear and dread are my life insurance."

—Erhard Loretan, underwriter of bold new routes in the Himalayas.

"Running risks is not obligatory to the game, but it's a part of it. Only a lengthy experience, enabling observations to be stored up both in memory and the subconscious, endows a few climbers with a sort of instinct not only for detecting danger, but for estimating its seriousness."

> —**Lionel Terray**

≍

"Do one thing every day that scares you."

> —Anonymous

≍

"I've had hornets up my shorts, been startled by a pigeon that brushed my face as it flew from its next, stuck my fingers into the belly of a bat in a thin crack, surprised a snarling raccoon behind a flake on a high ledge, and had my fixed rope chewed through by rats 2,500 feet up El Capitan. Welcome to nature."

> —**Don Mellor**

≍

"Play for more than you can afford to lose, then you will learn the game."

> —**Winston Churchill**, British prime minister during
>   World War II.

LOOKING BACK

"To those men who are born for mountains, the struggle can never end, until their lives end—to them it holds the very quintessence of living—the fiery core, after the lesser parts have been burned away."

—**Elizabeth Knowlton**

LOOKING BACK

For most climbers, their "storm years" (as Geoffrey Winthrop Young said) of accomplishment are in their youth. As hormonal fires and egos and youthful brass rage incandescently, an urge to transcend the ordinary and reach for the sky accounts for speed records in the Alps, solos of difficult routes, and the freeing of aid climbs. The exceptions to this are remarkable ascents at high altitude, where men and women stretch their endurance and continue achieving great ascents into their late forties.

There are climbers—such as Fritz Wiessner, Chris Bonnington, and Fred Beckey—who remain active until late in their lives, but even exceptional climbers such as these look back to their youth with wistfulness, while younger climbers speed by them, and they find themselves issuing the same conservative dogma (that once made them chafe) to younger partners. As Tom Patey, the Scottish iceman, sang it so well:

> Live it up, fill your cup, drown your sorrow
> And sow your wild oats while ye may
> For the toothless old tykes of tomorrow
> Were the Tigers of Yesterday.

It not unusual to meet burned-out climbers, tired of being broke, taking risks, and living as nomads. Then too, there are those who come to a realization that climbing was only a youthful phase. Yet no climber truly stops, in the sense that there are many levels to climb at, and many ways to remain active: giving up storm-blasted mountains for sun-baked rocks, settling for strenuous hikes instead of death-defying climbs, or simply living vicariously through the accounts of other more active climbers. More common perhaps are those who come to climbing later in their lives, and enjoy it as a relaxing, weekend avocation. But no climber, active or inactive, young or old, can help but look back to one of their earlier climbs with a sense that they had touched something beautiful and elusive, and found movement upon rock and ice as creation. Enduring friendships were discovered. New strengths were found. Horizons expanded. And all too often, the spectre of death was encountered—which, although unpleasant, gives climbers a context to accept death as they age or begin to lose their own family members. These experiences—loss, knowledge, strength, friendship—may have been passing moments, or month-long expeditions, but in these remembrances most climbers find necessary definition for the rest of their lives.

▲ ▲ ▲

"To find ways of getting more and more out of less and less."

—**John Gill,** at 54, describing how he began climbing
not just for sheer difficulty.

≍

"It's not the sixties. Use at least two bombproof anchors."

—**Steve Roper,** at Joshua Tree in the 1980s.

≍

"Yeah, so I could get to the Canadian Rockies before George
[Lowe] did."

—**Alex Lowe,** upon being asked whether he would
time travel, if it was possible.

≍

"The climbing world I knew nearly six decades ago was utterly
different from that of today. I'm fascinated to see what is now,
coming out of what was then."

—**Terris Moore,** in 1988.

≍

"Although the climb was rarely pleasurable it was nevertheless
unforgettable."

—**Ian McNaught-Davis,** on Peak Communism.

"One of the misfortunes of advancing age is that you get out of touch with the sunrise. You take it for granted, and it is over and done with before you settle yourself for the daily routine. That is one reason, I think, why, when we grow older, the days seem shorter, we miss the high moments of their beginning."

—**Lord Tweedmuir**

≍

"When one is young, one trifles with death."

—**Graham Greene,** prolific British novelist.

≍

"If I do a hard bolt route, it's nice, but the memory is short. If I climb a hard alpine route, the memory lasts forever."

—**Steve Haston,** British alpinist and all-rounder.

≍

"A mountaineer may be satisfied to nurse his athletic infancy upon home rocks, and he may be happy to pass the later years of his experience among the more elusive impressions and more subtle romance of our old and quiet hills. But in the storm years of his strength he should test his powers, learn his craft and earn his triumphs in conflict with the abrupt youth and warlike habit of great glacial ranges."

—**Geoffrey Winthrop Young**

"My humble Mecca. As we rode in I shared in imagination a little of the satisfaction of Burton, or of Manning when he reached Lhasa."

—**H. W. Tilman,** entering Namche Bazar in the
Khumbu Himalayas in 1950.

≍

"I have left and retired for good unless it becomes an Olympic sport and then I'd like to make a comeback."

—**Robyn Erbesfield**

≍

"A man's best moments seem to go by before he notices them; and he spends a large part of his life reaching back for them, like a runner for a baton that will never come."

—**David Roberts**

≍

"Civilization has stretched out its hand and changed it all, and though those who know the old days are somewhat sad that the old order has changed, yielding place to new, yet the new order is good, and the land of the great woods, lakes, mountains and rushing rivers is still mysterious enough to please anyone who has eyes to see, and can understand."

—**Norman Collie,** reminiscing on his many mountain
outings.

"I think a lot about climbing still, but not during the daytime. I think about it mostly at night, and on special occasions. I think about climbing when I am fed up with life in general. When I wish I could go over to the rocks or the trees. I enjoy my dreams about climbing."

> —**Fritz Wiessner** at 87, after a stroke stopped his climbing.

≍

"Looking back on those wild, free days in the open I realize that my happiest memories are of the suntanned faces of my old companions."

> —**Belmore Browne**

≍

"With a prolonged apprenticeship to mountaineering there comes not only a mastery of the craft itself, but such an acquaintanceship with all natural forces as must surely ripen into both love and awe. And, as the lover in mass commerce learns much not only of his mistress but of all women and of all mankind, so the mountaineer carries his experience of the beauty and the tenor of the great ranges to aid his enjoyment in his native hills. It is a mistake to suppose that there is any consolation for old age, or that the passage of years brings peace. There comes only partial resignation."

> —**Lord Schuster**

"It will not be long before the Alps once again become the terrible mountains of my youth, and if truly no stone, no tower of ice, no crevasse lies somewhere in wait for me, the day will come when, old and tired, I find peace among the animals and flowers."

—**Lionel Terray,** near his fortieth birthday.

≍

"I was born a hundred years too soon. We just had hemp rope, and we didn't even use that right."

—**Carl Blaurock,** at 98 years old (founding member of the Colorado Mountain Club).

≍

"Without doubt, the most important things have never been standing on a summit, or reaching a Pole. Unquestionably, it has been the work we have done in cooperation with the mountain people, establishing schools, medical clinics, and hospitals. Those are the things I will always remember."

—**Sir Edmund Hillary,** commenting on his Nepal work after he finished climbing.

≍

"If you're going climbing with young people, you get very, very used to seeing your climbing partner as a tiny little dot."

—**Chris Bonington,** in his fifties.

"Our era ended in 1967. It seemed like everyone was climbing big walls . . . that was when that runny-nosed, baby-faced
Bridwell kid came onto the scene."

    —T. M. Herbert

≍

"It is one of the greatest advantages of the sport that it can be
followed for so many years . . . the majority of the enthusiasts
hold on till the last, and it is no uncommon event to meet a
septuagenarian even on a difficult Swiss peak."

    —George D. Abraham

≍

"Here in Paris I dream of high hills."

    —Gaston Rébuffat

≍

"What if I live no more those kingly days? Their night
      sleeps with me still.
I lift my feet upon the starry ways; My heart rests in the hill.
I may not grudge the little left undone;
I hold the heights, I keep the dreams I won."

    —Geoffrey Winthrop Young

"I should say that a man who, after a boyhood apprenticeship on smaller hills, began serious mountaineering at the age of eighteen, would not reach anywhere near full powers until he was thirty-five (supposing that he had three weeks every year in the hills). . . . It is not rare for men of sixty or more to climb first-class peaks in the Alps. They will go slower than a younger party, but I doubt whether they will be much more tired at the end of the day. I am certain that they will have performed technically with greater competence and economy and that they will have appreciated the climb at least as deeply."

—**Douglas Busk**

≍

"Vy can't ve chust climb!"

—**John Salathé**

≍

"I'd rather wear out then rust out."

—**Dick Bass,** on seeking adventure in his sixties.

≍

"There's still time, but there ain't forever."

—**Rick Sylvester**

"The greatest moments of life are very apt to fall singularly flat. We manage to discount all their interest beforehand, and are amazed to find that the day to which we have looked forward so long—the day, it may be, of our marriage, or ordination, or election to be Lord Mayor—finds us curiously unconscious of any sudden transformation and as strongly inclined to prosaic eating and drinking as usual. At a later period we may become conscious of its true significance, and perhaps the satisfactory conquest of this new pass has given us more pleasure in later years than it did at the moment."

—**Sir Leslie Stephen**

≍

"I haven't had so much fun in thirty-seven years."

—**Tom Frost,** 60, climbing El Cap's Nose in 1997 (he made the second ascent in 1960) with his son.

OUTSIDERS

"The ordinary man looking at a mountain is like an illiterate person confronted with a Greek manuscript."

   —**Aleister Crowley**

OUTSIDERS

For the purposes of this chapter, "outsiders" are those who are not climbers and because of their own misconceptions or awe of steep places, let along the act of climbing—their words have correspondingly amused or inspired the old hands of climbing. A lot of this awe or mistaken impressions about climbing no doubt stems from colonial conceptions about the dark dangers that resided in the hinterlands. For example, a seventeenth century writer described New Hampshire's Presidentials as, "mountains daunting terrible, being full of rocky hills, as thick as Molehills in a Meadow, and cloathed with infinite thick Woods." No small wonder then that some remnant and ancestral fear of dragons still remains in our consciousness.

Today, climbing—along with base jumping, drop kayaking, spelunking, and upskiing—might remain one of the most misunderstood or feared pastimes in North America. This results in general confusion about the game in the mainstream media. It also means that the non-climbing public is left with the sort of poorly researched copy as generated by a Jeep advertisement in a recent magazine: "Rocky Mountain spikers [not part of the lexicon] will argue that Duray [sic], near Crested Butte, Colo. . . . [actually near Telluride] provides ice climbers the top thrill [instead of *challenge*]." Needless to say, no one comes out ahead with this sort of commercial: the unknowing public continues to think of climbing as a crazed thrill seeker's pursuit, while climbers themselves will probably abstain from buying Jeeps.

Add to this churlish ad copy those stories generated by editors on deadline at magazines and newspapers—the sort of venues that many people read to be informed—and most readers end up knowing less about climbing than before the article. This might be changing with the recent avalanche of carefully reported stories about the 1996 Everest disaster. But even in the best of circumstances, this education is taking place only gradually.

Hollywood is also responsible for spawning an array of misconceptions about climbing. Take, for example, its comic book styled climbers in *Cliffhanger,* stilted clichés in *K2,* and the former assassin-climber turned art professor in *The Eiger Sanction.* During the filming of the latter movie, the star Clint Eastwood met two real-life heroes descending from a record ten-hour ascent of the mountain's notorious North Face. That particular night saw one of the most bizarre reversals of conventional adulation, with Clint Eastwood looking like the fawning fan standing beside the real superstars, Peter Habeler and Reinhold Messner.

But mixed within the discombobulated words of the media, the lay public, and adoring autograph hounds there are those other outsiders' words of awe. For instance, the nineteenth-century naturalist John Burroughs was not an alpinist, but he had the sensibility to provide the following sort of textured response to mountains: "It is always worthwhile to sit or kneel at the face of grandeur, to look up into the placid faces of the earth gods and feel their power."

Since time immemorial, Burroughs was not alone. Other writers, composers, and philosophers have looked up to mountains and cliffs and felt extraordinary inspiration or repulsion, even if they—John Ruskin, Johann Wolfgang von Goethe, Richard Wagner, Percy Bysshe Shelley, J. R. R. Tolkien, Kahlil Gibran, or D. H. Lawrence—never set foot upon the heights.

"One day you'll go climbing and stop before your slippers do."

—Italian peasant shouting out to Reinhold Messner.

≍

"It is not overly romantic to say that the marriage between experienced hikers and Mount Washington is a torrid affair."

—New Hampshire newspaper editor, after climbing
deaths occurred on that mountain.

≍

"When a woman hunts for a partner she is instinctively looking for one who would provide her with a good strong gene pool. . . . If he has a tendency to hang from cliffs by his fingertips . . . it's a pretty safe bet that he's fit and healthy."

—*Cosmopolitan*

≍

"It is exactly that of a bull in the arena. Confused and tormented by something far beyond their understanding, they react to the sight of a cliff as the bull to a cape. Not knowing why, they charge."

— *San Francisco Chronicle* letter to the editor
explaining a widely publicized El Capitan climb.

"At fifty miles high, Mount Kilimanjaro is Africa's highest mountain."

> —*Barrie Banner* newspaper, Ontario.

≍

"I tried to climb it twice, it tried to kill me twice. Look, if that target's trying to climb the Eiger, chances are my work will be done for me."

> —Clint Eastwood's assassin role, from *The Eiger Sanction.*

≍

"Could we have your autograph?"

> —Girl scouts to Chip Woodland after they watched him climb the North Face of Robson in a storm.

≍

"I thought you died years ago, so let me congratulate you!"

> —From a fan's letter to Sir Edmund Hillary, after a newspaper story about his pulmonary edema.

≍

"She climbed the last 2000 feet Saturday morning, emerging onto the summit around noon into view of other campers."

> —*The Denver Post* describing Alison Hargreaves's solo and oxygen-bottle-free ascent of Everest.

"Mountain climbing, once the sport of Edmund Hillary and other gentlemanly types, has today become rock climbing. And a few elite athletes have turned that into 'free' climbing—scaling near-vertical mountain faces without the aid of ropes."

—*Popular Science*

≍

"Should we have the right to climb ice?"

—**George Smith,** sportswriter for *The Times Leader* in Wilkes-Barre, PA, after a man slipped on a hiking trail and fell off a cliff.

≍

"St. Elias has a fascination for mountain climbers because no one has perched as yet upon its topmost ridge. To the joys of stumbling among rocks, hanging over the edges of precipices, slipping and falling upon ice and snow, and freezing between times, it promises to add the ecstasy of pioneering. Relatively considered this is certainly something. If the ambition to stumble and fall and freeze is incomprehensible to most people, everyone will understand the desire to do what has never been done before, even if it excites no very great sympathy."

—Newspaper reporter in 1897.

"Never known for self-restraint, Kerri seeks a companion who can help her tie up her loose ends."

—From a *Hustler* pictorial of a naked woman holding a rope tied onto a cliff.

≍

"One other very important question I have is are there firearms allowed in the park as for protection and does one need to technically climb—ropes and gromets [sic]—or can one hike to the summit of Mt. McKinley? My last question is, is Mt. McKinley usually covered with snow around the first of June?"

—Prospective climber's letter to Denali national park rangers.

≍

"It is the necessity of human nature that practical records should be broken; and to affect the inability to understand why men are irresistibly attracted to the chance of doing something first or going somewhere first, is a waste of time. They are built that way, and to the very impulse that rules them the world is enormously indebted."

—*New York Times* writer covering George Leigh Mallory's "Because it's there" statement.

"Climbing walls can be any height from 7.5 meters to 15 meters. The discipline is basically the opposite of the more-publicized rappelling, which is the art of descending sheer walls."

—*Jerusalem Post,* May 21, 1995.

≍

"I wouldn't go over there if I were you. They steal from the store and they smell and they wear rags and even piss right outside their tents. I tell you, it's like a leper colony that place."

—Yosemite Lodge worker to a woman getting ready to visit the Camp 4 climber campground.

≍

"The earth is like a beautiful bride who needs no manmade jewels to heighten her loveliness but is content with the green verdue of her fields, and the golden sands of her seashores, and the precious stones on her mountains."

—**Kahlil Gibran**

≍

"She Knows the Nose: The Goal Was To Climb Alone Along the Prow of El Capitan in Yosemite Without Ropes, and Hill Was the First."

—*L.A. Times* headline about Lynn Hill's freeclimbing the Nose in 1994.

"Mountains are to the rest of the body of the earth, what violent muscular action is to the body of man. The muscles and tendons of its anatomy are, in the mountain, brought out with force and convulsive energy, full of expression, passion, and strength."

—**John Ruskin**

≍

"It is a magnet for men who dream, a magnet for men who should know better. A teasing lady who often is no lady, McKinley lures and seduces. It flirts with men who can't say no to its beauty. It crushes men who respond to the invitation, but stay too long."

—**Lewis Freedman,** from his book, *Dangerous Steps.*

≍

"Thou hast a voice, great Mountain, to repeal
Large odes of fraud and woe; not understood
By all, but which the wise, and great, and good
Interpret, or make felt, or deeply feel."

—**Percy Bysshe Shelley**

≍

"Separate from the pleasure of your company, I don't much care if I never see another mountain in my life."

—**Charles Lamb's** 1801 letter to William Wordsworth.

"Those piton spikes you use have shortened the life expectancy of the Totem Pole by fifty-thousand years."

 —Navajo man to rock climber.

≍

"We just went from foothold to foothold; our toupees made it impossible to see more than a foot or two above our heads."

 —Evelyn Waugh

≍

"Above the summit of the mountains we saw a light which we could not explain. It was clear and without lustre, like the light of the Milky Way, yet more dense, something like the Pleiades, but much greater. We gazed up at it continually, until, changing our position we beheld it as a huge pyramid, pervaded by some inward mystic light, something like that of a glowworm, rising far above the dark mountaintops. We then saw it as the vast summit of Mont Blanc."

 —Goethe

≍

"Let me create more works like those which I conceived in that serene and glorious Switzerland, with my eyes on the beautiful gold-crowned mountains; they were masterpieces and where else could I have conceived them."

 —Richard Wagner

"The Alps were alike beautiful in their snow and their humanity and I wanted neither for them nor for myself sight of any throne in Heaven but their rocks and of any spirits in Heaven but their clouds."

—**John Ruskin**

≍

"The ultimate goal of someone deeply involved in mountaineering is to climb the seven summits—the highest mountain of each continent. I have one down and six to go."

—**Araz Yacoubian**

≍

"I can't do with mountains at close quarters, they are always in the way, and they are so stupid, never moving and never doing anything but obtrude themselves."

—**D. H. Lawrence**

≍

"No, that cannot be. No one has ever been there. It is impossible."

—A Turkish abbott's reply in 1876 to James Bryce, who mentioned that he had just climbed 16,946-foot Mount Ararat.

WHY CLIMB?

"It is not the goal of grand alpinism to face peril, but it is one of the tests one must undergo to deserve the joy of rising for an instant above the state of crawling grubs."

—**Lionel Terray**

WHY CLIMB?

Lionel Terray is peerless for his dismantling of the universal climbing question: "Why?" In his book, *Conquistadors of the Useless*, he never took such a rhetorical question head-on. Instead, he shared his experiences, without pretension, and by using his shrewd and brusque charm. It is one of the best climbing books ever written if only because when Terray went on a good climb, he wrote with direct and unadorned prose about his experience. His book title itself was as much ink as he cared to spend on the philosophy of why; it was simply *Useless*. But later, in a journal article that he wrote about his first ascent of Alaska's Mount Huntington, Terray left us with a quote that is frequently parroted, in one form or another, throughout the exclusive hangs—the boulder fields and bars, the huts and backcliffs, the magazines and the books—when he wrote about "rising above . . . crawling grubs."

Terray's forty-year-old, epigrammatic answer is typical of the modern active climber, versus the nineteenth-century patrician, who expounded in grander philosophic terms, and left us with a trove of philosophical musings about the splendors of nature, the joys of camaraderie, or the need to strengthen a nation. The modern activist, unlike the gentlemanly climber of yesteryear, is too impatient to muse over nature, often solos, and is usually apolitical. So there is a distinct divergence of philosophy on the subject of why we climb.

There is in fact a book of climber profiles entitled *Why I Climb*, but its subjects, either due to their own reticence or the interviewer's politeness, delivers us no closer. Ask the question yourself sometime among a party of climbers, and count the variety of evasions the question engenders. Most often, climbers simply circle the question with a defensive version of: "If you have to ask why you won't understand the answer," or a variety of half-cocked, fanatical, theological, or philosophically immature (yet hilarious) replies.

Indeed, the gallant George Leigh Mallory started the whole furor after a long Philadelphia lecture by saying "Because it's there" as a quick rejoinder to get a reporter off his back. Some philosophers believe that Mallory was trying to show that the mountain had form and presence, that it was a sentient being with a cosmic life force. But Mallory then wrote again and again about why he climbed, often without Zen overtones, and two more of his more profound reasons are contained herein.

Then there is Jeff Salz—published (and forgotten) in a 1970s *Ascent* journal. After his climbing partner died on Fitzroy, Salz wrote that "the commitment of the mountaineer is to pursue wholeheartedly to know whole-soulfully the man-shaped essence that he is." A man who was unsympathetic to climbing, sitting next to Salz on his airplane ride home from Patagonia, badgered Salz about why he climbed. Salz's reply identified the basics (and the futility) of why he climbed as well as anyone before or since:

"What you do on your own scale for your own soul is all that matters. I don't have to do things that other people may consider as difficult anymore. To climb a mountain to see if I can keep from falling off is no reason. To climb a mountain to celebrate my limbs, the sky, my friends, seems better. . . . I wish to fulfill myself in dance not words. Walking skillfully along the top of the world we may receive a priceless vista of our lives and see that which is truly important to us. We may never be able to make sense of why this is so, and if our discoveries are great they always seem to defy words."

▲ ▲ ▲

"The Love of Mountains is Best"

—Pre-1558 Greek inscription on the summit of
Niesen, Switzerland.

≍

"Contact! Contact!"

—**Henry David Thoreau,** climbing Katahdin.

≍

"From early days, I found that climbing was the only thing in
life that gave more than momentary satisfaction."

—**Dougal Haston**

≍

"For the sake of bodily exercise and the delight of the spirit."

—**Conrad Gesner**

≍

"To search for community."

—**Roger Klein**

≍

"We are made for it."

—**Gaston Rébuffat**

"One reason is never given openly, rather is disguised and hidden and never even allowed in suggestion, and I venture to think it is because it is really the inmost moving impulse in all true mountain-lovers, a feeling so deep and so pure and so personal as to be almost sacred, too intimate for ordinary mention. That is, the ideal joy that only mountains give—the unreasoned, uncovetous, unworldly love of them we know not why, we care not why, only because they are what they are; because they move us in some way which nothing else does . . . and we feel a world that can give such rapture must be a good world, a life capable of such feeling must be worth the living."

—F. W. Bourdillon

≍

"I have loved climbing, and the reason is that if you are up there and having a beautiful day and everyone is clicking and a few cumulus clouds are sprinkled around and everyone is moving and handling the rope right and the air is clear and you can see forever, well, I think that is really almost an unmatchable experience. It is almost sacred."

—Glenn Exum

≍

"You don't see farmers as climbers. You see city people. Farmers don't need to climb."

—Yvon Chouinard

"As a kid, I knew two things to be self evident. Flying: Believe it and it'll happen. Superpowers: Bound to be something—spinach or whatever will do the trick. Climbing is my flying and coffee is my spinach."

—**Peter Croft**

≍

"I find that rock climbing is the finest, most healthiest sport in the whole world. It is much healthier than most; look at baseball, where 10,000 sit on their ass to watch a handful of players."

—**John Salathé**

≍

"To those who have struggled with them, the mountains reveal beauties that they will not disclose to those who make no effort. That is the reward the mountains give to effort. And it is because they have so much to give and give it so lavishly to those who will wrestle with them that men love the mountains and go back to them again and again. The mountains reserve their choice gifts for those who stand upon their summits."

—**Sir Francis Younghusband**

≍

"Because it is so entirely irrational."

—**Anonymous**

"Some also have wished that the next way to their Father's House were here, that they might be troubled no more with either hills or mountains to go over: but the way is the way, and there is an end."

—**John Bunyan**

≍

"But we little know until tried how much of the uncontrollable there is in us, urging across glaciers and torrents, and up dangerous heights, let the judgment forbid as it may."

—**John Muir**

≍

"Yes, if there was enough money in it. But not just for sport."

—**Billy Taylor,** when asked if he would climb Denali again, after his 1910 climb to the North Peak.

≍

"Something of our personality has gone into every mountain on which we have spent our strength and on which our thoughts have rested, and something of its personality has come into ours and had its small effect on everything that has come within our influence."

—**R. L. G. Irving**

"I cannot well argue with such detractors from what I consider noble sport. No more argument is possible than if I were to say that I liked olives, and someone asserted that I really eat them only out of affectation. My reply would be simply to go on eating olives; and I hope the reply of mountaineers will be to go on climbing Alps."

—Sir Leslie Stephen

≍

"We glory in the physical regeneration which is the product of our exertions; we exult over the grandeur of the scenes that are brought before our eyes, the splendors of sunrise and sunset, and the beauties of hill, dale, lake, wood, and waterfall; but we value more highly the development of manliness, and the evolution, under combat with difficulties, of those noble qualities of human nature: courage, patience, endurance, and fortitude."

—Edward Whymper

≍

"It is to conquer fear that one becomes a climber. The Climber experiences life to its extreme. A climber is not crazy. He is not out to get himself killed. He knows what life is worth. He is in love with living."

—Walter Bonatti

"For I have said that the medium of some men is paint or stone or boats or a schoolroom, or poems or paper and ink; that of a few is rocks and snow and the uphill movement of limbs."

—**Wilfrid Noyce**

≍

"Because it is the natural thing to do."

—**Tom Patey**

≍

"A cure for baldness."

—**Jon Krakauer**

≍

"I suppose the first sight of a mountain is always the best. Later, when you are waiting to start, you may grow to hate the brute, because you are afraid. And when, finally, you are climbing, you are never aware of the mountain as a mountain: it is merely so many little areas of rock to be worked out in tens of handholds, footholds and effort, like so many chess problems. But when you first see it in the distance, remote and beautiful and unknown, then there seems some reason for climbing. That, perhaps, is what Mallory meant by his 'Because it's there'."

—**A. Alvarez**

"Deep within us I think we know that we need challenge and danger, and the risk and hurt that will sometimes follow. 'Dangerous' sports would not be as popular as they are if this were not so. Mountain climbing is not the only way of dealing with an over-organized, over-protective society. But it is one good way."

—**Woodrow Wilson Sayre**

≍

"He is lucky who, in the full tide of life, has experienced a measure of the active environment that he most desires. In these days of upheaval and violent change, when the basic values of today are the vain and shattered dreams of tomorrow, there is much to be said for a philosophy which aims at living a full life while the opportunity offers. There are few treasures of more lasting worth than the experience of a way of life that in itself is wholly satisfying. Such, after all, are the only possessions of which no fate, no cosmic catastrophe can deprive us; nothing can alter the fact if for one moment in eternity we have really lived."

—**Eric Shipton**

≍

"If you don't scale the mountain, you can't view the plain."

—Chinese proverb.

"I am being driven forward
Into an unknown land.
The pass grows steeper,
The air colder and sharper.
Wind from my unknown goal
Stirs the strings
Of expectation.
Still the question:
Shall I ever get there?
There where life resounds,
A clear pure note
In the silence."

—**Dag Hammarskjöld**

≍

"If you wish to see the valleys, climb to the mountain top;
If you desire to see the mountain top, rise into the cloud;
But if you seek to understand the cloud, close your eyes and
think."

—**Kahlil Gibran**

≍

"Because I'm grumpy when I'm not climbing."

—**Doug Scott,** to two frostbitten climbers inside an
igloo.

"It's a long way from thile Benvyn to the Himalayas, where you can enjoy the finest mountain adventure of all. The mountains and the hills are there to be discovered; and whether they are thile boy's crags of heather, or the great ranges untrodden since they were made, always they entice us to know them, to master all that bars the way; to them a part of us belongs. Always they speak to us of what is beyond them, and beyond the grasp of our minds; and once we have seriously played with them we can never let them be."

  —Charles Evans

≍

"To sit on rocks, to muse o'er food and tell
To slowly trace the forest's shady scene,
Where things that own not man's dominion dwell
And mortal foot hath ne'er or rarely been;
To climb the trackless mountain all unseen.
This is not solitude, 'tis but to hold converse
with nature's charms, and see her stores
untolled."

  —Lord Byron

≍

"Because we're insane."

  —Warren Harding

"But if adventure has a final and all embracing motive it is surely this:

We go out because it is in our nature to go out to climb mountains and to sail the seas, to fly to the planets and plunder into the depths of the oceans. By doing these things we make touch with something outside or behind, which strangely seems to approve our doing them. We extend our horizon, we expand our being, we revel in the mastery of ourselves which gives an impression, mainly illusory, that we are masters of the world. In a word, we are men and when man ceases to do these things, he is no longer man."

—Wilfrid Noyce

⋈

"To share the experience with other people with the same goal."

—Bradford Washburn, to a newspaper reporter in 1949.

"I like to be with my husband."

—Barbara Washburn, to the same reporter, after becoming the first woman to climb Denali.

"What we get from this adventure is just sheer joy. And joy is after all, the end of life. We do not live to eat and make money. We eat and make money to be able to enjoy life. That is what life means and what life is for."

    —**George Leigh Mallory**

≍

"Our hearts overflowed with an unspeakable happiness."

    —**Maurice Herzog,** who, with Louis Lachenal, first
       climbed an 8,000-meter peak (Annapurna).

≍

"To lose weight."

    —**Bryan Becker,** with his mouth full of food, after his
       first ascent of the Hallucinogen Wall, to a television
       journalist.

≍

"To feed the rat."

    —**Mo Anthoine**

≍

"Climbing gives me something that a female can give me. I feel a great comfort, a completeness there that's almost orgasmic."

    —**Mark Wilford,** from the film *Cloudwalker.*

"Climbing is a metaphor for life itself. There is the aspiration and the uncertainty, the journey and the risk, the success and its concomitant satisfaction. Life on the wall becomes a simplified model of life in the harried world, a model with equal anguish, but one whose challenges are carved into perfect definition. We win here and we know that we can win elsewhere."

—**Don Mellor**

≍

"Maybe Himalayan climbing is just a bad habit, like smoking, of which one says with cavalier abandon, 'must give this up someday, before it kills me.'"

—**Greg Child**

≍

"So if you cannot understand that there is something in man which responds to the challenge of this mountain and goes out to meet it, that the struggle is the struggle of life itself upward and forever upward, then you won't see why we go."

—**George Leigh Mallory**

WHO'S WHO

Abraham, George D. 1872–1965, Author of *British Mountain Climbs, The Complete Mountaineer, Modern Mountaineering, Mountain Adventures, On Alpine Heights and British Crags.*

Abruzzi, Duke of Italian nobleman who first climbed Mount St. Elias (Alaska) in 1897, attempted to reach the North Pole, authored numerous Ruwenzori first ascents, and climbed high on K2 in 1909.

Afanassieff, Jean Known for his climbing in the Alps in the 1970s and the first Frenchman to summit Everest.

Allison, Stacy Active American rock climber and mountaineer.

Alvarez, A. British journalist and author of *Feeding the Rat*, a biography of Mo Anthoine.

Anker, Conrad Member of the North Face team, with ascents in Antarctica and Alaska.

Anthoine, Mo 1939–1989, Noncomformist British climber with a reputation for toughness, who died of a brain tumor in 1989.

Backes, Scott American alpinist.

Balmat, Jacques Scientist who first summited Mont Blanc in 1786.

Barber, Henry "Hot Henry" was known for a spate of visionary rock climbs throughout the 1970s, most notably his 1971 on-sight solo of Yosemite's Steck-Salathé.

Barry, John British climber known for such climbs as Deborah's East Ridge (Alaska) and the North Face of the Eiger, and author of *K2: Savage Mountain, Savage Summer*, and numerous instructional texts.

Bass, Dick Owner of Snowbird Ski Area in Utah who became known to business executives everywhere for his mid-age climbing escapades through the book, *Seven Summits*.

Batard, Marc French speed climber who climbed Everest in twenty-four hours.

Bates, Bob American climber most renowned for climbing high on K2 in 1938 and in 1954, and for his books, *The Love of Mountains Is Best* and *Mountain Man* (a biography of Belmore Browne).

Beck, Eric Yosemite rock climber from the 1960s.

Beckey, Fred The most prolific mountaineer in North America; author of *Mountains of North America,* and *The Challenge of the North Cascades.*

Beidleman, Neil Ultramarathoner, rock climber, mountain guide, and aerospace engineer, who has climbed a new route on Denali and made a twenty-four-hour ascent of Makalu.

Bell, J. H. B. Scottish 1920s climber; author of *A Progress in Mountaineering.*

Blanchard, Barry Canadian alpinist and UIAGM guide renowned for his tolerance of the rotten rock and steep waterfall ice of the Canadian Rockies.

Blaurock, Carl Founding member of the Colorado Mountain Club and first to climb all of that state's fifty-four 14,000-foot-plus peaks.

Boardman, Peter 1950–1982. British alpinist who disappeared on Everest with Joe Tasker; author of *The Shining Mountain* and *Sacred Summits.*

Bonatti, Walter Italian alpinist, known for his solo ascents in the Alps. Author of *The Great Days* and *On the Heights.*

Bouchard, John American alpinist and owner of Wild Things equipment company.

Boukreev, Anatoli Phenomenal athlete and mountain guide who climbed numerous 8,000-meter peaks without oxygen, and was criticized for not using it during the 1996 Everest disaster—in which he saved several lives. He died in an avalanche on Annapurna in 1997.

Bourdillon, F. W. British doctor who developed the closed-circuit oxygen system for the 1953 Everest climb.

Breashears, David American rock climber, initially known for his bold ascents in Colorado, who went on to become an Everest filmmaker.

Breitenbach, Jake American climber killed on Everest in 1963.

Bridwell, Jim Legendary Yosemite climber who applied his techniques to steep walls around the world.

Bristow, Lily Nineteenth-century British climber who espoused guideless climbing in the Alps.

Brown, Katie Sixteen-year-old superstar competition climber.

Browne, Belmore Artist and Alaskan explorer who came to within two hundred feet of the summit of Denali in 1912.

Bruce, General 1866–1939, Leader of 1922 and 1924 Everest expeditions; author of *Himalayan Wanderer.*

Buhl, Hermann 1925–1957, Austrian alpinist who made the first ascents of Broad Peak and Nanga Parbat (solo); author of *Nanga Parbat Pilgrimage.*

Buhler, Carlos Accomplished American climber in the Himalayas.

Bunyan, John 1628–1688, Author of *The Pilgrim's Progress.*

Burgess, Alan Expatriate Brit and Himalayan climber.

Burlingham, Frederick British author of *How to Become an Alpinist.*

Burroughs, John Nineteenth-century American naturalist.

Calhoun, Kitty American alpinist and first woman to summit Makalu by the difficult French Ridge.

Camus, Albert French author, 1879–1965.

Carpé, Allen American climber who launched onto technical difficulties before their time; killed in a crevasse fall on Denali in 1932.

Casarotto, Renato 1948–1986, Accomplished Italian soloist killed by a crevasse fall beneath K2.

Cassin, Riccardo Italian alpinist most known for leading the first ascent of K2 and climbing the South Face of Denali.

Cesen, Tomo Yugoslavian alpinist whose solos of Jannu and Lhotse were disputed.

Chevalley, G. Swiss coauthor of *Forerunners to Everest: The Story of Two Swiss Expeditions of 1952.*

Child, Greg Expatriate Australian, now American, with wide-ranging big wall and Himalayan accomplishments; author of *Thin Air,* and *Mixed Emotions.*

Chouinard, Yvon Influential American big wall and ice climber. Founder of Patagonia and author of *Climbing Ice.*

Conway, Sir Martin 1856–1937, British author of *The Alps, The Bolivian Andes,* and *Climbing and Exploration in the Karakorum Himalayas.*

Cook, Frederick American explorer turned hoax perpetrator, who temporarily convinced the world that he climbed McKinley and reached the North Pole. Author of *To the Top of the Continent* and *My Attainment of the Pole.*

Cowles, Betsy Active American climber in the 1930s. Accompanied Houston and Tilman during the first southern reconnaissance of Everest in 1950.

Croft, Peter Humble American rock soloist and master of the enchainment.

Crowley, Aleister Turn -of-the-century British occultist and alpinist.

Curran, Jim British filmmaker and author of *K2: Triumph and Tragedy.*

Davidson, Art American 1960s climber, active in Alaska, and mostly known for his 1967 winter ascent of Denali. Author of *Minus 148.*

de Saussure, Horace Bénédict 1740–1799, Swiss scientist who climbed Mont Blanc in 1787; author of *Voyages dans les Alpes.*

DeCamp, Eric French alpinist.

Destivelle, Catherine Former French champion sport climber who turned to bold solos and free climbing in the big mountains.

Dittert, René Swiss coauthor of *Forerunners to Everest: The Story of Two Swiss Expeditions of 1952.*

Donini, Jim American alpinist with wide-ranging accomplishments in Alaska.

Drummond, Ed American rock climber and author of *A Dream of White Horses*.

Du Faur, Freda New Zealand alpinist, first women's ascent of Mount Cook, 1910.

Dumal, Rene French author of the mountaineering satire, *Rum Doodle*.

Dunn, Robert American journalist who accompanied Frederick Cook on his first expedition to McKinley; author of *The Shameless Diary of an Explorer*.

Edwards, John Menlove 1910–1958, British cragsman and schizophrenic, see *Menlove: The Life and Writings* and *Sampson*.

Emerson, Ralph Waldo 1803–1882, American philosopher and essayist.

Emmons, Arthur Member of epic 1932 first ascent of China's Minya Konka; coauthor of *Men Against the Clouds*.

Epperson, Greg American rock climber and photographer.

Erbesfield, Robyn Former top American contender of the world sport climbing circuit.

Erickson, Jim Influential American rock climber, soloist, and author of *Rocky Heights*.

Evans, Charles British author of *Eye on Everest*, *Kanchenjunga the Untrodden Peak*, and *On Climbing*.

Everett, Boyd Wall Street broker who methodically ticked off Alaskan ascents in the 1960s until his death on Dhaulagiri; author of *The Organization of Alaskan Expeditions*.

Exum, Glenn Teton guide known for his first ascent of the Exum Ridge.

Fischer, Scott American guide (owner of Mountain Madness) killed on Mount Everest in 1996.

Franklin, Scott American sport climber who first repeated the 5.14 rock climb "To Bolt or Not To Be."

Genet, Ray Swiss expatriate who started the successful guide business on Denali and was killed on Everest.

Gesner, Conrad 1516–1565, Swiss climber, philosopher, and scientist.

Gill, John Mathematician and gymnast who perfected the art of bouldering; see his biography, *Master of Rock.*

Goethe, Johann Wolfgang von 1749–1832, German philosopher and writer.

Goss, Wayne Colorado climber known for his first winter ascent of the Diamond in 1967.

Grissom, Colin American doctor and climber.

Habeler, Peter Austrian mountain guide and partner of Reinhold Messner (both of whom pioneered Everest without oxygen) author of *Lonely Victory.*

Hall, Rob New Zealand mountain guide who was killed while accompanying a sick client down Everest in 1996.

Harding, Warren American rock climber famous for first climbing El Capitan's Nose in 1958.

Hargreaves, Alison British soloist who climbed Everest without oxygen and was killed on K2.

Harrer, Heinrich Austrian who first climbed the North Face of the Eiger and Mount Hunter's West Ridge; author of *Seven Years in Tibet* and *The White Spider.*

Haston, Dougal 1940–1977, British alpinist killed skiing by an avalanche; author of *In High Places* and *Calculated Risk.*

Hawthorne, Nathaniel Nineteenth-century American novelist.

Hechtel, Richard German who first climbed Mont Blanc's Peuteray Ridge.

Hemming, Gary 1934–1970, American climber famous for his beatnik lifestyle and first ascents in the Alps.

Herbert, T. M. 1960s Yosemite rock climber and humorist.

Herzog, Maurice In 1950 he summited Annapurna and lost most of his fingers and toes; went on to become sports minister of France; author of the classic *Annapurna.*

Higgins, Molly American rock climber who climbed in the Pamirs during the disastrous season of 1974.

Hill, Lynn American rock climber and former world champion sport climber who has elevated rock climbing to new levels, particularly after free climbing El Capitan's Nose in a day in 1994.

Hillary, Sir Edmund New Zealand climber who first climbed Mount Everest in 1953, then built schools and hospitals throughout Nepal; author of *Ascent, High Adventure,* and *Nothing Venture, Nothing Win* .

Hong, Steve American physician and rock climber.

Hornbein, Thomas American physician and rock climber most well-known for his bold first ascent and traverse of Everest in 1963.

Houston, Charles The grandfather of American high-altitude medicine, who engineered the first ascent of Nanda Devi in 1936, the first ascent of Foraker, and early American attempts on K2.

Hunt, Sir John Leader of the 1953 Everest expedition and author of *The Ascent of Everest.*

Hunter, Diana The original female phenom of rock climbing. She died while soloing Rocky Mountain National Park in 1975.

Irving, Robert L. G. British author of *The Alps, A History of British Mountaineering, The Matterhorn, The Mountain Way,* and *The Romance of Mountaineering.*

Javelle, Emile 1847–1883, British author of *Alpine Memories.*

Johnston, Dave Long-time Alaskan mountaineer, best known for his 1967 winter ascent of Denali.

Kain, Conrad Austrian alpine guide who settled in Canada and pioneered numerous alpine ascents, often with clients in tow.

Kennedy, Michael Canadian/American alpinist, with numerous Alaskan ascents; former publisher of *Climbing* magazine.

Knowlton, Elizabeth American climber who attempted Nanga Parbat in 1932, and author of *The Naked Mountain.*

Kor, Layton Prolific American stonemason, who climbed the Eiger Direct in winter and scores of bold new routes throughout the American West.

Krakauer, Jon American alpinist renowned for his bold solo of the Devils Thumb in Alaska; author of *Eiger Dreams* and *Into Thin Air.*

Lacelle, Guy Accomplished Canadian water-ice soloist.

Lachenal, Louis Chamonix guide killed in a crevasse fall, 1955; the little-known partner of Maurice Herzog during their first ascent of an 8,000-meter peak (Annapurna).

Long, Jeff American climber and author of climbing novels, *Angels of Light* and *Ascent.*

Loretan, Erhard Swiss climber who became famous for his 24-hour ascent of Everest from the North.

Lowe, Alex American thought to be the best all-around climber in the world.

Lowe, George American cousin of Jeff, famous for bold alpine ascents.

Lowe, Jeff American innovator of ice climbing and visionary alpine ascents; author of *Ice World.*

MacCarthy, Albert Famous for leading the 1925 first ascent of Mount Logan.

Mallory, George Leigh 1886–1924, originally slated for Holy Orders, then lost on Everest; famous for saying "Because it's there."

McCarthy, Jim American 1960s rock climber, lawyer, and former president of the American Alpine Club.

McNaught-Davis, Ian British rock climber and satirical essayist.

Meade, C. F. British author of *Approach to the Hills.*

Mellor, Don American professional climbing guide and instructor; author of *Climbing in the Adirondacks* and *The Trailside Guide to Rock Climbing.*

Messner, Reinhold Tyrolian alpinist first to complete the "race for all fourteen 8,000-meter peaks" in 1986 and innovator of innumerable bold, often solo alpine ascents; the most influential climber in history; author of *Crystal Horizon* and *The Seventh Grade.*

Metcalf, Peter American alpinist and C.E.O. of Black Diamond Equipment Company in Utah.

Moffat, Gwen British climbing guide and author of *Space Below My Feet.*

Montague, Charles E. 1867–1928, British author of *Action and Other Stories.*

Moore, Terris American who completed first ascent of Minya Konka; author of *Mount McKinley: The Pioneer Climbs.*

Muir, John 1810–1882, American naturalist and mountaineer; author of *The Mountains of California, The Yosemite,* and *Stickeen.*

Mummery, Albert F. British alpinist and rock gymnast, killed on Nanga Parbat in 1895; author of *My Climbs in the Alps and Caucasus.*

Murray, W. H. Scottish author of *The Scottish Himalayan Expedition, The Story of Everest,* and *Undiscovered Scotland.*

Nietzsche, Friedrich 1844–1900, German philosopher and author of *Thus Spake Zarathustra,* and *Birth of Tragedy.*

Norgay, Tenzing Nepalese who accompanied Hillary to the top of Everest; subject of *Tiger of the Snows.*

Norman, Collie 1858–1929, British alpinist and author of *Climbs & Exploration in the Canadian Rockies* and *Climbing on the Himalaya and other Mountain Ranges.*

Noyce, Wilfrid 1917–1962, British alpinist and author of *Mountains and Men, Snowdon Biography, South Col: One Man's Adventures on the Ascent of Everest.* Killed while climbing in the Pamirs.

O'Douglas, William American Supreme Court justice and lover of mountains who wrote *Of Men and Mountains.*

Okonek, Brian Alaskan climber and owner-guide of Alaska-Denali Expeditions.

Ölz, Oswald Austrian physician and frequent partner of Reinhold Messner.

Osius, Alison Accomplished American rockclimber and senior editor of *Climbing* magazine. First woman president of the American Alpine Club; author of *Second Ascent*.

Parker, Herschel American scientist who defrocked Frederick Cook's 1907 claimed ascent of Denali. Parker himself was forced to turn around two hundred feet shy of the summit in 1912.

Patey, Tom Scottish alpinist and physician who died rappelling from a seastack; author of *One Man's Mountains*.

Peck, Anne Smith 1850–1935, American alpinist who made an early ascent of Huascaran Norte, and author of *A Search for the Apex of America*.

Petrarch Italian poet who was one of the first (non-Asians) to champion the joys of the mountains after his ascent of Mount Ventoux in 1335.

Piana, Paul American climber who freed the Salathé Wall in Yosemite in 1989; author of *Big Walls: Breakthroughs on the Free-Climbing Frontier*.

Pratt, Chuck 1960s American rock climber, famous for his skill with crack climbs.

Raeburn, Harold British author of *Mountaineering Art*.

Raleigh, Duane Editor of *Climbing* magazine.

Randall, Glenn American alpinist and author of *Breaking Point*.

Rébuffat, Gaston French climber who participated in the 1950 ascent of Annapurna; author of *Starlight and Storm, Between Heaven and Earth, On Ice and Snow and Rock,* and *Mont Blanc to Everest.*

Reichardt, Lou American scientist and Himalayan climber; former president of the American Alpine Club.

Ridgeway, Rick American alpinist and filmmaker, owner of Adventure Photo agency, and author of *Seven Summits, The Last Step,* and *The Boldest Dream.*

Robbins, Royal Influential American rock climber who applied Yosemite big-wall climbing techniques to alpine rock around the world; author of *Rockcraft.*

Roberts, David Pioneer of Alaskan climbs and respected American climbing writer; author of *The Mountain of My Fear, Moments of Doubt,* and *Deborah: A Wilderness Narrative.*

Roskelley, John The most accomplished American Himalayan climber of the 1970s and 1980s; author of *Last Days* and *Nanda Devi.*

Ruskin, John 1819–1900, British art critic and writer.

Rutkiewicz, Wanda Accomplished Pole who climbed a half dozen 8,000-meter peaks before disappearing high on Kanchenjunga.

Sacherer, Frank Early free-climbing juggernaut of Yosemite Valley who was killed while climbing in the Alps.

Salathé, John The 1950s master of Yosemite.

Sayre, Woodrow Wilson American philosopher who led a clandestine alpine-style attempt on Everest in the early 1960s; author of *Four Against Everest.*

Schoening, Pete American who made the first ascent of Hidden Peak and whose famous ice ax belay saved his companions' lives on K2 in 1953.

Scott, Doug British climber who, after climbing Everest siege-style in 1975, mastered lightweight alpine-style ascents of other Himalayan giants throughout the 1980s; author of *Big Wall Climbing* and *Himalayan Climber.*

Seidman, Dave American climber known for his first ascent of Denali's South Face, killed on Dhaulagiri in 1967.

Sella, Vittorio Italian alpinist, companion of the Duke of Abruzzi, and world's first mountain photographer.

Shipton, Eric British explorer and frequent companion of H. W. Tilman, who espoused lightweight mountain travel, author of *The Six Mountain Travel Books.*

Simpson, Joe British alpinist most known for his classic accident, told in his *Touching the Void;* also author of *This Game of Ghosts.*

Smythe, Frank 1900–1949, British alpinist and author of *The Adventures of a Mountaineer, Camp Six: An Account of the 1933 Mount Everest Expedition,* and *Climbs in the Canadian Rockies.*

Steck, Allen American known for his 1965 first ascent of Mount Logan's Hummingbird Ridge; coeditor of *Ascent,* and an active rock climber into his seventies.

Stephen, Sir Leslie 1832–1904, British climber, theologian, father of Virginia Woolf, and author of *The Alps.*

Stevenson, David American climber and professor of English at the University of Illinois.

Stump, Mugs Maverick American famous for his first ascent of the East Face of the Moose's Tooth and various solo climbs; killed in a freak crevasse fall on Denali in 1992.

Sylvester, Rick American rock climber famed for jumping off cliffs in James Bond movies.

Tabei, Junko Japanese "housewife" who made the first woman's ascent of Everest in 1975, and first woman's ascent of the Seven Summits in 1992.

Tabin, Geoff American ophthalmologist, former columnist for *Penthouse*, ascensionist of the Seven Summits, and author of *Blind Corners*.

Thoreau, Henry David Nineteenth-century American philosopher and naturalist; author of *Walden*.

Tilman, H. W. The last real British explorer of the twentieth century, who made the first ascent of Nanda Devi in 1936, took up sailing in his fifties, and was lost at sea as a seventy-nine-year-old.

Tolkien, J. R. R. American author of the *Lord of the Rings* trilogy.

Tonella, Guido Italian journalist and mountaineer.

Twight, Marc Nietzschean American climber who made a spate of fast ascents in the Alps and the Canadian Rockies.

Uemura, Naomi 1941–1984, Humble Japanese climber who, after climbing Everest, sought to become the first to climb the highest summits on each continent, but disappeared on his solo winter climb of Denali.

Ullman, James Ramsey American author of *Straight Up* and *The White Tower*.

Underhill, Miriam First American woman to espouse guideless climbing; author of *Give Me the Hills*.

Unsoeld, Willi 1926–1979, American philosopher and climber best known for his ascent of the West Ridge of Everest in 1963; killed in an avalanche on Mount Rainier.

Venables, Stephen First British climber to summit Everest without oxygen, in 1989, via the difficult Kangshung Face; author of *Painted Mountains; Everest: Alone at the Summit;* and *Himalaya Alpine Style.*

Viesturs, Ed Frequent American Everest climber seeking to climb all fourteen 8,000-meter peaks; to date he has climbed ten.

Washburn, Barbara First woman to climb Alaska's Mount Hayes, Denali, Marcus Baker, and Berthoud.

Washburn, Bradford Husband of Barbara; "Mr. McKinley," and world-renowned cartographer and photographer; coauthor of *The Conquest of Denali.*

Waterman, John Mallon Disturbed solo climber known for his 148-day solo of Mount Hunter's difficult Southeast Spur; disappeared on Denali during solo attempt of new route, 1982.

Waugh, Evelyn 1903–1966, British humorist and prolific author and travel writer.

Webster, Ed Prolific American cragsman who turned to Everest climbing; director of American Alpine Club Press; author of *Rock Climbs in the White Mountains of N.H.*

Wellman, Mark American paralyzed in climbing accident who went on to climb Half Dome and El Capitan; author of *Climbing Back.*

Whillans, Don British wit who summited Annapurna and espoused beer drinking as a means of staying fit.

Whitehouse, Annie Participant in various Himalayan expeditions: Annapurna, Dhaulagiri, Everest, and Ama Dablam.

Whymper, Edward 1840–1911, British alpinist who first ascended the Matterhorn; author of *Scrambles Among the Alps, Chamonix and the Range of Mont Blanc,* and *Travels Amongst the Great Andes of the Equator.*

Wickwire, Jim Lawyer who bivouacked just below the summit of K2 in 1978 and survived.

Wiessner, Fritz Although he came up short in his attempt to summit K2 in 1939, he established a plethora of classic rock routes (such as Waddington and Devils Tower), and pioneered climbing in the Gunks.

Williams, Bob Colorado climber who, along with John Gill, raised the art of bouldering in the 1960s and 1970s.

Williamson, Jed Former president of the American Alpine Club.

Wordsworth, William English poet, 1770–1850.

Wunsch, Steve Made many extreme first ascents in Colorado, New York, and Great Britain. In 1974, he put up one of the hardest routes in the world: Super Crack in the Gunks.

Young, Geoffrey Winthrop 1876–1958, British climber whose sage advice influenced an entire generation of climbers and whose loss of a leg in World War I did not stop him from climbing; author of *Mountaincraft* and *On High Hills.*

Younghusband, Sir Francis 1863–1942, British soldier and author of *The Epic of Mount Everest.*